Cooking in Real Life

Cooking in Real Life

DELICIOUS & DOABLE RECIPES FOR EVERY DAY

Lidey Heuck

PHOTOGRAPHY BY DANE TASHIMA

SIMON
ELEMENT

NEW YORK LONDON TORONTO SYDNEY NEW DELHI

An Imprint of Simon & Schuster, Inc.
1230 Avenue of the Americas
New York, NY 10020

First Simon Element hardcover edition March 2024

SIMON ELEMENT is a trademark of Simon & Schuster, Inc.

Simon & Schuster: Celebrating 100 Years of Publishing in 2024

For information about special discounts for bulk purchases, please contact Simon & Schuster Special Sales at 1-866-506-1949 or business@simonandschuster.com.

The Simon & Schuster Speakers Bureau can bring authors to your live event. For more information or to book an event, contact the Simon & Schuster Speakers Bureau at 1-866-248-3049 or visit our website at www.simonspeakers.com.

Interior design by Laura Palese

Manufactured in China

10 9 8 7 6 5 4 3 2 1

Library of Congress Cataloging-in-Publication Data has been applied for.

ISBN 978-1-6680-0215-5
ISBN 978-1-6680-0216-2 (ebook)

To my mom and dad, for encouraging me
to write my own story.

Contents

Foreword

Ina Garten

I like to say that when Lidey Heuck came to work for me right out of college, she was so young that she still had shell on her. When most young people were out looking for a job—*any* job— Lidey was looking for her dream job. She found someone who knew someone who knew me, and she sent me her resume. Fortunately, at that moment, I happened to be looking for a creative person to help me with social media.

A few weeks later, Lidey arrived in East Hampton for an interview, not just with her resume in hand but also with an entire social media program that was simple and brilliant. I was really impressed. We spoke for a while and I remember asking myself, *Am I going to love her?* My final question in that interview was "What makes you crazy?" And she said, "When my house-mates don't keep the kitchen clean." I hired her on the spot.

> Lidey subscribes to the same theory of home cooking that I do.

Lidey had little cooking experience when she arrived, but she was like a sponge, soaking up everything I could teach her about cooking, entertaining, flower arranging, and the business of writing books and filming a television show. In fact, her enthusiasm really awakened in me a love for teaching, for which I'm very grateful to her. I adore teaching a young person what I've learned and then sending them out into the world to find their own way.

Over the next seven years, we did everything together—shopping, testing recipes, answering customers' cooking questions, social media, print media, and book tours. But the thing Lidey and I both enjoyed the most was cooking together: the process of figuring out a recipe, testing it a dozen times, and tweaking the ingredients and the process along the way. It was great fun to build our ideas together and come out with a dish that was better than either one of us. The best days were the ones when we would go from testing recipes during the day to our regular Monday night bridge club!

Somewhere in the middle of those seven years, Lidey slowly began to fly on her own; she was making wonderful suggestions, such as what to add to a soup to make the flavors pop. One recipe in particular, my Boston Cream Pie, we actually worked on together for several *years*. I had been telling Christina Tosi from Milk Bar that the cake needed something, but I couldn't figure out quite what. She suggested that I pour a "soak" or a syrup over the cake before it was assembled. I made one with the usual water, sugar, and orange juice, which was nice, but something was still missing. Lidey suggested that we add Grand Marnier—and bingo! The cake was perfect! The student teaches the teacher. It was so satisfying for me to watch the transformation.

And now Lidey is flying on her own. This book is not only gorgeous and so informative for both new and experienced cooks but it's also filled with recipes you'll want to make every day. Lidey subscribes to the same theory of home cooking that I do. We all want recipes that have ingredients you can buy in almost any grocery store, recipes that are easy enough to make without breaking a sweat and will be delicious and satisfying for either an ordinary weekday dinner or for a special occasion. Lidey has mastered the fundamentals of cooking so well, and with this book, she has also found her own style. I'm beyond proud of her. And, as I wondered in that original interview, I did fall in love with her, and so will you.

Introduction

When I first showed up to work for Ina Garten, just two weeks after graduating from college, I wore a pencil skirt and ballet flats. My corporate attire was a dead giveaway that I had no idea what my job would really entail. I knew I was there to help Ina grow her social media platforms, which seemed like enough of an office job to dress the part, but what I didn't realize was that I'd also be helping to shop for recipe ingredients, popping out to the garden to pick cherry tomatoes or fresh rosemary, and before long, cooking alongside the Barefoot Contessa herself.

Unbeknownst to me, I was on a course that would bring me here—more than ten years later—to the introduction of my own cookbook.

It didn't take me long to catch the recipe bug. Ina's innate understanding of what people want to eat and the way she invents recipes that make people excited to cook fascinated me. I was inspired by watching her take a recipe from the spark of an idea to a complete, perfected dish, and by the way she could make a familiar favorite feel new again. And of course, I loved getting to be a part of the process—testing, tasting, and retesting each recipe, and the satisfaction of finally nailing a particularly tricky one.

I began playing around with my own recipes at home, practicing techniques I'd learned at work, like roasting chicken breasts on the bone, or making a simple buttercream frosting. I tested my recipes late on weeknights and cooked for friends, and my now-husband, Joe, on the weekends.

> The measured precision of Ina's kitchen combined with my off-road cooking adventures were a perfect education.

The measured precision of Ina's kitchen combined with my off-road cooking adventures were a perfect education. At work, I learned how to create a foolproof recipe—how to write clearly and succinctly, how to get the most flavor out of the fewest ingredients, how to elevate a dish with a sprinkle of fresh herbs or flaky sea salt.

At home I learned other lessons, often the hard way: how to time dinner so the chicken is done long before 9 p.m., how *not* to freeze a bottle of Champagne, and how to make hosting easier by asking friends to bring an appetizer or dessert. I learned not to strive for perfection in the kitchen, but rather to embrace the fact that mishaps are part of the process, and part of life.

Over the years, through my work as a recipe contributor to the *New York Times*, prep cook under Erin French at The Lost Kitchen in Freedom, Maine, chef for a busy family of five, and virtual cooking class teacher, I've been in a unique position to observe what people want to eat and how they like to cook. Every comment, email, or social media message I receive provides instant feedback and insight, reminding me that regardless of age, location, and situation, we all want pretty much the same thing when it comes to cooking at home.

We want dishes that are inventive but not overly complicated, food that's healthy but not boring, and recipes that use familiar ingredients but encourage us to do things a little bit differently. We want to get as much done in advance as possible. We appreciate serving suggestions and permission to make substitutions. And we want cook-pleasing and crowd-pleasing recipes, whether we are cooking for ourselves or a group, on a busy weeknight or a holiday.

This is cooking in real life.

I didn't set out to have a career in food, but I was exposed to home cooking—or, rather, the spectrum of it—growing up.

I didn't set out to have a career in food, but I was exposed to home cooking—or, rather, the spectrum of it—growing up. I am the middle child between two brothers, and when we were kids, both of my parents worked for a newspaper in Pittsburgh. My dad edited the business section, and Mom was a film critic and then covered cultural events, often working in the evening. Dinners at our house were simple and to the point. (To this day my mom jokes, "I may not be a good cook, but I'm a fast cook.") She made broiled salmon, broiled chicken, and the occasional hard-shell taco with ground beef. My dad made enormous pots of "leftovers soup," which my brothers, Sam and Henry, and I not-so-secretly dreaded. We had a lot of frozen dinners and pizza nights, too.

Sunday dinners at my grandparents' house were another story. The whole extended family would gather for drinks and an elaborate spread of cheese, cured meats, and dips in the living room, while my grandfather put the finishing touches on dinner. I liked to sit on a little stool in the corner of the kitchen, taking in the smell of garlic and the steam rising from big pots of tomato sauce or simmering braised meat. Two of my uncles owned restaurants in Pittsburgh, including a wood-fired pizza joint and Lafôret, a critically acclaimed French restaurant. They'd be in the kitchen, too, happy to show me how to make a roux with butter and flour or teach me how to hold a glass of wine, long before I was old enough to have one myself.

When dinner was ready, the adults gathered around the dining room table, and the cousins around the kids' table. There was lots of talking and laughing and big platters of food being passed back and forth. My grandfather would make sausage and peppers, or lasagna, or spaghetti Bolognese, sprinkled with a few shavings of the "family cheese," an ancient hunk of Parmesan he inherited from his Italian mother and kept in the freezer. My brothers and cousins and I would slather butter onto thick slices of bakery white bread, a rare treat we did not have at

home, and sneak away from the table for an impromptu wrestling match. But we always made it back in time for my aunt Candy's chocolate soufflé cake (see Candy's Flourless Chocolate Cake [page 211]).

Even then, I think I understood that good food could make an occasion out of nothing.

I also saw the equally valid, functional side of cooking at home—which is that days are long, and when you have three kids and a dog to feed, it's not always about making something over the top. Sometimes, getting a home-cooked meal on the table is a victory in itself.

What I'm interested in today is the golden middle ground where joy and practicality meet—that's what I mean by "delicious and doable" recipes. My goal in writing this book is to share recipes that will meet you where you are. I want to give you plenty of ideas for turning simple salads or soups into full, satisfying meals, or reinventing last night's dinner into today's lunch. I want to help you take shortcuts when you need them and find ways to elevate your cooking when you want a meal to feel extra special. I want to give you a collection of recipes as varied as the reasons and occasions for which we cook.

There are recipes for weeknight dinners like Salmon with Honey & Chili Crunch (page 122) and Saucy Shrimp alla Vodka (page 118), which deliver big flavor in a short amount of time.

There are recipes that make the most of colorful, seasonal produce in a way that's simple and accessible, such as Skillet Apple Crisp with Shortbread Crumble (page 218), Baked Crab Dip with Sweet Corn and Old Bay (page 41), and Escarole Salad with Cara Cara Oranges, Marcona Almonds & Goat Cheese (page 57). I'm inspired by seasonal ingredients but not bound by them—strawberries might be at their best in June, but that doesn't mean I don't eat them in February. I've noted when in-season produce is particularly important to a dish but for the most part, you can make these recipes anytime.

And finally, when the occasion calls for something celebratory, there are showstopper dishes like Braised Short Ribs with Port, Shallots & Cranberries (page 111), Champagne Chicken (page 88), and Rainbow Sprinkle Ice Cream Cake (page 213), for kids and grown-up kids alike.

The recipes in this book are written with you—the shopper, chopper, and dish-doer—and the people around your table in mind. They recognize that life is full of both quotidian and special moments, and mostly times in between. They all call for uncomplicated food that is delicious and satisfying—food makes our time both in the kitchen and at the table more enjoyable. These are recipes I use in my real life, and I hope they'll soon be regulars in yours, too.

XOX
Lidey

GETTING
STARTED

Making the Recipes

The Fine Print

I always recommend reading the introductory paragraphs above a recipe, as well as the ingredients list and instructions, before you get started. We've all had that moment in the middle of making a recipe when we realize the chicken we want to serve in two hours needed to marinate overnight. Whoops! Reading the recipe all the way through before you head to the grocery store is the best way to avoid surprises along the way.

The Notes

Many of the recipes have little notes on the sides of the page. I hope they help you customize the recipes, cook more efficiently, and provide some serving inspiration. I've broken them into the following categories for easy reference as you flip through the book.

MAKE IT A MEAL

The formula of protein-vegetable-starch isn't as relevant to the way we eat as it used to be. Dinner might be grilled steak with veggies and potatoes, but it could also be a bowl of soup with toasted bread, or a big salad with a piece of last night's chicken on top. The recipes are organized to provide a useful way to navigate the book, but I hope you'll feel free to make and eat these dishes whenever you like, however you like. Along the way, I've noted lots of ways to turn smaller dishes into complete meals with the addition of a protein, grain, or super-simple side dish. The Easy Add-Ons chapter (page 260) provides simple "no-recipe recipes" for some of these basics, such as Seared Salmon Fillets (page 262) and Basic Roasted Potatoes (page 263), and there are even more serving ideas in Menus (page 266) if you're looking for inspiration or planning something special.

SIMPLE SWAP

Having lived in rural Maine and the Hudson Valley, I know it's not always easy to find specific ingredients. I keep this in mind when writing recipes and avoid using hard-to-find ingredients. I also know there are times we'd rather use something we have on hand than make a special trip to the store. Whenever possible, I've suggested good alternatives, as well as substitutions for dietary reasons. I hope this helps you find ways to make the recipes in this book work for your family.

GET AHEAD

On busy weekdays, and when you're hosting family and friends, it's helpful to get much of the cooking done in advance. No matter which recipe you're making, there are ways to plan ahead, whether it's chopping vegetables, making a sauce, or assembling a full dish you can pop into the oven when the time is right. When a recipe is particularly well suited to being made in advance, I've made a "Get Ahead" note, so you can get organized—whether that means being a calm, collected host or fitting weeknight dinner prep into your busy schedule.

COOKING FOR A CROWD

With weeknight cooking in mind, most of the recipes in this book serve 4 to 6 people. But in real life, there are many times we need to scale things up for larger gatherings. While not all recipes can be easily doubled, I've made notes on dishes that are particularly suited to doubling and indicated when a few slight tweaks are in order.

LEFTOVERS FOR LUNCH

When I hear the word "leftovers," I immediately think of old Thanksgiving turkey and cranberry sauce, which, if I'm honest, are not my favorite. But planning ahead and finding creative and delicious ways to use leftovers can be a great time-saving tool. Throughout this book, I've included notes on the recipes I like to double for a satisfying lunch the next day, or ways to repurpose leftovers that make them feel "new" again.

TIPS

These are the catchall tips I've included whenever I think a particular cooking technique or ingredient in a recipe needs a little more explanation.

Pantry Primer

Notes on a few basic ingredients that make a big difference.

KOSHER SALT

Not all salts are made alike. I've tested all of the recipes in this book with Diamond Crystal kosher salt, which has a coarser grain and milder flavor than iodized table salt. Diamond Crystal brand is the "chef's standard" and is even comparatively milder than other kosher salts. You should be able to find it in the baking aisle of most large grocery stores. If you use iodized table salt, sea salt, or another brand of kosher salt, start with less than the recipes call for to avoid over-seasoning.

FLAKY SEA SALT

While kosher salt is my go-to for everyday seasoning, I occasionally use a flaky sea salt when I want to finish a dish with a salty crunch, or in desserts when I want to see just a hint of salt on the surface of a baked good. There are many brands of flaky sea salt, but my two favorites are Jacobsen and Maldon.

BLACK PEPPER

You'll notice many of my recipes call for "a few grinds of freshly ground black pepper." In most cases, I don't call for specific amounts, because I think everyone has a different preference when it comes to black pepper. But I do highly recommend using a pepper grinder to grind as you go—and avoiding the preground stuff—for the freshest flavor.

CHICKEN BROTH

Nothing beats homemade chicken broth. While I do have an easy recipe for making chicken broth with a leftover roast chicken (see page 259), most of the time I just use store-bought broth. I always call for low-sodium broth (both chicken and vegetable) in my recipes, because the salt content can vary drastically from brand to brand.

OLIVE OIL

There are so many different kinds of olive oil, it can be hard to know which one to use. You don't need to buy the most expensive olive oil on the shelf to make delicious food. As long as the bottle says "extra-virgin" olive oil, you should be good to go. If you like, you can use a fancier oil for dipping bread, or drizzling on tomato salads, but I've made all these recipes with plain old EVOO and it always does the trick for me.

BUTTER

I use unsalted butter in both my savory and sweet recipes. As with chicken broth, brands of salted butter vary, so using unsalted is the best way to keep an eye on the amount of salt going into a dish. The only exception to this rule is when I buy fancy butter to serve with bread. Salted cultured butter at room temperature is one of life's sublime treats.

10 Tools for Better Cooking

1. SHARP KNIVES

As a cook, your knives are your most important tools. While you don't need fancy knives to make delicious food, keeping your knives sharp will help you enormously. A sharp chef's knife makes chopping an onion, or slicing cucumbers, or removing the skin from a piece of salmon, so much easier AND safer. It may seem counterintuitive, but you're much more likely to cut yourself with a dull knife than a sharp knife, because the knife can easily slip while you're working. There are lots of different knife sharpeners you can buy, some high tech and some as simple as sharpening the blade on a stone. Many hardware and cookware stores can also do it for you.

2. OVEN THERMOMETER

I can't stress enough how important it is to have a thermometer in your oven! (Thank you to Ina for teaching me this!) It'd be great if our ovens heated to the temperature we set them to, but in real life, many ovens (even brand-new ones!) can be surprisingly inaccurate. This is crucial for baking but also affects the way meat and vegetables roast. Keeping a thermometer in your oven is the best way to make sure your oven is at the right temperature, regardless of what the dial says. Oven thermometers are inexpensive and sold at most hardware stores, kitchen stores, and online.

3. PLASTIC CUTTING BOARDS

I have a stack of 8 × 11-inch white plastic cutting boards that I use for chopping and prepping everything. (I know, I know, plastic.) But they're the only cutting boards I can run through the dishwasher, which I do often to clean and sanitize them. They're my kitchen workhorses, and unlike wooden boards, are maintenance-free. Above all else, they are *the* tool that helps me keep a clean and efficient kitchen. My favorite plastic cutting boards have one side that grips the counter, so they don't slide around while you chop.

4. HUGE METAL MIXING BOWLS

I used to have a funny habit of always choosing mixing bowls that were ever so slightly too small for whatever I was doing, and then having to use two bowls instead of one. I think I was trying to avoid having to wash a big bowl, only to have to wash two! Then, I discovered the enormous metal mixing bowl. It's lightweight, it's inexpensive, and it's bigger than you need it to be for most tasks. But when you're making a big salad, tossing a double batch of pasta, or straining a batch of chicken broth, you'll wonder how you ever lived without one of these.

5. KITCHEN SCISSORS

You probably have a pair of scissors in your kitchen, but if you're also using them to open mail, I highly recommend buying another pair that you just use for cooking. Kitchen shears come in handy often, but especially when working with raw meat and chicken. I find it's just nice to have a mental separation between these scissors and the ones I'm using to open Amazon packages, you know? Being able to throw them in the dishwasher is key, so look for a pair that's stainless steel or otherwise marked dishwasher safe.

6. DIGITAL SCALE

You'll notice in the dessert section of this book that I give both volume measurements (cups, tablespoons) as well as weight measurements (in grams.) And in some savory recipes, I mention weight, too. Using a scale might sound like overkill for a home cook, but it's really just an easy way to double-check ingredient amounts and ensure accuracy with tricky-to-measure ingredients like flour and brown sugar. And with baking, it can save you a sinkload of dishes, too.

7. MANY, MANY MEASURING SPOONS

This one sounds simple, and it is! You know how it's kind of annoying to have to rinse a table-spoon you threw in the sink because you thought you were done with it? Or worse, when you reach for the measuring spoons only to remember they're in the dishwasher, mid-cycle? One little ring of teaspoons is technically enough to get through a recipe, but if you cook or bake often, consider buying a few extra sets. It's a little luxury that will save you a lot of time in the long run.

8. MEAT THERMOMETER

There are a few different ways to tell if a piece of chicken or fish is cooked through. Chefs may be able to tell doneness just from a quick press on the surface of the fillet or piece of chicken, but more likely, you might need to cut into the piece to see how it looks. For new or nervous cooks, the easiest way to check if a piece of meat is cooked through is to use an instant-read thermometer (and even for experienced cooks, using a thermometer can provide peace of mind).

9. QUARTER SHEET PANS

Sheet pan recipes get a lot of love for being easy, but if I'm being honest, there are few things I dread more in the kitchen than washing a giant sheet pan. Who's with me? Sometimes, it's unavoidable, but if I'm cooking one piece of fish, a smaller amount of vegetables, or baking off a few balls of cookie dough, I love having a quarter-sheet pan as an option. It measures only 9 × 13 inches and can also fit into smaller half-ovens. Oh, and it's so much easier to wash!

10. RESTAURANT-GRADE KITCHEN TOWELS

I'm always trying to use fewer paper towels in the kitchen, but when you cook as much as I do, it's not easy! I did pick up a little restaurant trick during my stint at The Lost Kitchen that's made a huge difference. I ordered a big pack of inexpensive, restaurant-grade kitchen towels and use them for everything: wiping up the counter, doing dishes, you name it. Then, I just toss them in the wash. They get stained, used, then stained again, and that just means they're doing their job. As for the pretty dish towels, I save those to use as hand towels, or as a cute accessory for my oven door handle.

RECIPES

Snacks
& Drinks

Spicy Paloma Punch 22

Golden Beet Dip with Yogurt & Tahini 26

Baked Harbison (Fondue for Real Life!) 29

Cider & Bourbon Old-Fashioned 30

Honey Roasted Cashews *with a Kick* 33

Beach Water 34

Brown Bread Crackers with Crème Fraîche
& Smoked Salmon 37

Gin Martini with Rosemary & Grapefruit 38

Baked Crab Dip with Sweet Corn & Old Bay 41

Garibaldi Spritz 42

Cherry, Nectarine & Jalapeño Salsa 45

Spicy Paloma Punch

4 cups freshly squeezed
grapefruit juice (about
8 grapefruits, see Tip)

1 (750 ml) bottle good-quality
tequila blanco or reposado

¾ cup freshly squeezed lime
juice (about 6 to 8 limes)

⅔ cup strained Jalapeño
Simple Syrup (recipe follows
on page 25)

1 grapefruit, quartered and
thinly sliced crosswise, for
serving

1 lime, thinly sliced, for serving

Ice, for serving

1½ cups unflavored sparkling
water

12 to 14 slices candied
jalapeño (from the simple
syrup), for serving

A batch cocktail mixed up in a pitcher makes any gathering, big or small, feel like a party. And not only that, it's practical—you can serve a special cocktail without having to shake or stir another round of drinks every time someone's ready for a refill.

This particular punch is inspired by one of my favorite cocktails, the paloma, which is simply tequila, grapefruit soda or juice, and fresh lime. My version adds jalapeño simple syrup for a nice kick. As with a spicy margarita, that hint of heat makes for a slightly more complex and oh-so-satisfying drink.

1. In a large glass pitcher or punch bowl, combine the grapefruit juice, tequila, lime juice, and simple syrup and mix well. Add slices of grapefruit and lime to the pitcher and store, covered, in the fridge until you plan to serve the drinks (see Get Ahead).

2. Serve the punch in ice-filled glass tumblers, topped with a splash of sparkling water, a piece of candied jalapeño, and a slice of lime or grapefruit from the pitcher, for garnish.

TIP

If you have the patience to squeeze grapefruits (or friends to help), go for it, but if not, bottled juice is absolutely fine. If possible, use a flash-pasteurized grapefruit juice like Uncle Matt's Organic or Natalie's if you can—it's the closest you can get to freshly squeezed juice without the squeezing.

GET AHEAD

The simple syrup can be made up to 48 hours in advance. Fresh citrus juice is always best the day it's squeezed, but you can make the base for this punch several hours in advance and store it in the refrigerator before serving.

RECIPE CONTINUES

JALAPEÑO SIMPLE SYRUP

Makes 1½ cups

1 cup thinly sliced jalapeño peppers (3 to 4 medium peppers)

1 cup granulated sugar

1. In a small saucepan, combine 1 cup water and the jalapeños and bring to a boil over high heat. Reduce the heat to low, add the sugar and stir until it's completely dissolved. Simmer the syrup for 5 minutes over medium heat, until slightly reduced. Set aside for at least 1 hour to cool completely.

2. Store in a sealed container in the refrigerator. Remove the candied jalapeños after 1 hour and store separately until you're ready to use. The longer the peppers sit in the syrup, the spicier the syrup will be.

Golden Beet Dip with Yogurt & Tahini

MAKES 1 PINT

1 pound golden beets, trimmed and scrubbed (about 6 medium beets)

1 tablespoon extra-virgin olive oil, plus more for drizzling

1 medium garlic clove

½ cup plain whole-milk Greek yogurt (5 ounces)

⅓ cup tahini

2 tablespoons freshly squeezed lemon juice (1 lemon)

2 teaspoons maple syrup

1½ teaspoons kosher salt

½ teaspoon ground turmeric

Pinch of cayenne pepper

Fresh mint leaves, for serving (optional)

Toasted pita, or fresh vegetables, such as sliced cucumbers, scrubbed radishes, celery, peeled or baby carrots, or any other vegetables, for serving

I make this recipe so often that my husband, Joe, jokingly refers to it as our "house dip." Made with roasted beets, tahini, and Greek yogurt, it's the perfect creamy dip to eat with crudités, toasted pita, or even baby carrots straight from the bag. Golden beets are sweeter and milder in flavor than red beets, and a little bonus: they won't stain your hands and cutting board bright pink!

1. Preheat the oven to 400°F.

2. Place the beets on a large piece of aluminum foil and drizzle them with the olive oil. Roll the beets around gently to make sure they are coated in oil, then wrap the foil around them to form a sealed packet.

3. Place the packet on a sheet pan and roast until the beets are tender when pierced with a fork, 45 minutes to 1 hour. Set aside until cool enough to handle, then peel the beets and discard the skins.

4. In a food processor, combine the beets and garlic and pulse until coarsely chopped. Add the yogurt, tahini, lemon juice, maple syrup, salt, turmeric, and cayenne and process until smooth, 10 to 15 seconds.

5. Transfer to a small serving bowl. Garnish with a drizzle of olive oil and a few mint leaves, if using. Serve with pita and crudités. This dip will keep for up to 5 days in the refrigerator.

SIMPLE SWAP

If all you can find are red beets, you can use them here, too—the beet flavor will just be slightly more pronounced.

LEFTOVERS FOR LUNCH

I like using leftover beet dip as a sandwich spread or spooning some onto a grain bowl or salad.

Baked Harbison (Fondue for Real Life!)

SERVES 4 TO 6

1 (9-ounce) wheel Harbison cheese (see Tip)

1 tablespoon dry white wine

1 tablespoon kirsch (cherry brandy)

Kosher salt

Whole nutmeg, for serving

Crushed pink peppercorns, for serving (optional)

Sliced baguette, for serving

One winter weekend, Joe and I road-tripped with some friends to Cape Cod to take chilly beach walks and cozy up by the fire. I thought it would be fun to do a fondue night, so I went out one morning, searching for Appenzeller and Emmentaler—the traditional cheeses used in Swiss fondue. I picked up some cherry brandy, and then spent the afternoon grating cheese and prepping and dicing all the different things I'd bought to dip. I didn't have a fondue pot so I kept the cheese hot in a double boiler. By the time we sat down to eat, it was late. Everyone was generously served in the cherry brandy department and in need of more than just cheese for dinner. And while the fondue was delicious, it had been an all-day affair. I decided there must be an easier way to bring melty cheese to the people.

It turns out, there is! Harbison, from Vermont-based Jasper Hill Farm, is one of my favorite cheeses to use on a cheese board. It's rich, creamy, and mildly tangy. Harbison is a treat at room temperature, but baked until soft, it's transcendent. In this recipe, I add a splash of kirsch and white wine to the cheese, along with a pinch of grated nutmeg and pepper, for the full Swiss fondue treatment. This is way easier to make and, dare I say, even more delicious than the real deal.

1. Preheat the oven to 375°F.

2. Unwrap the paper from the cheese and carefully cut the top rind (or the bottom—whichever is peeking out more from the bark). Place the bark-wrapped cheese cut-side up in a baking dish just large enough to hold it.

3. Pour the wine and kirsch over the cheese and sprinkle with salt. Bake until the cheese is hot and bubbling on top, 15 to 20 minutes, spooning any liquid in the pan over the cheese halfway through.

4. Carefully transfer the baking dish to a hot pad. Garnish with freshly grated nutmeg, a generous pinch of salt, and a pinch of pink peppercorns, if using. Serve hot with the sliced baguette.

TIP

Harbison is sold at cheese shops and grocery stores nationwide, and you can also order directly from Jasper Hill Farm. I tried this recipe with a number of other cheeses, but only Harbison's unique bark wrapping keeps the cheese from falling apart in the oven.

Cider & Bourbon Old-Fashioned

MAKES 2 DRINKS

4 ounces (½ cup) fresh apple cider

4 ounces (½ cup) bourbon

1 teaspoon maple syrup

4 dashes bitters, plus more to taste

Ice cubes, for serving

2 (2-inch) strips orange peel, for serving

Apple cider and bourbon are a match made in heaven, and like any great couple, they bring out the best in each other. In this spin on a classic old-fashioned, apple cider complements bourbon's caramel and vanilla notes, and the bourbon adds an edge to the cider's sweetness. With a drizzle of maple syrup, a dash of bitters, and an orange twist, the aroma of this drink alone is enough to transport you to the crispest, leaves-falling, flannel-shirt day of your dreams.

1. Place two rocks glasses in the freezer to chill while you make the drinks.

2. In a large mixing glass, combine the apple cider, bourbon, maple syrup, and bitters. Add 1 cup ice and stir gently for about 10 seconds.

3. Place one large ice cube, or a handful of regular-size ice cubes, into the chilled glasses. Strain the cocktail into the glasses, then garnish each drink with an orange twist and serve immediately.

TIP

Regular ice works just fine in this recipe, and for any drink served on the rocks, but if you enjoy making cocktails at home, consider buying some jumbo silicone ice molds. Big ice cubes and spheres have less surface area, which means they melt more slowly and won't dilute your drinks. Not to mention, having giant ice cubes in your freezer is a majorly impressive party trick.

COOKING FOR A CROWD

To make a batch of 6 cocktails, multiply the recipe by 3. Combine the ingredients in a pitcher and wait to add ice until just before serving.

Honey-Roasted Cashews *with a Kick*

MAKES 6 CUPS

2 large egg whites

½ cup light brown sugar

2 tablespoons honey

2 tablespoons unsalted butter, melted and slightly cooled

1 teaspoon kosher salt

¼ teaspoon cayenne pepper

1 pound unsalted, roasted cashews (about 4 cups)

Flaky sea salt, for sprinkling

These crunchy cashews are the perfect little snack to have with drinks. Roasted with honey, brown sugar, and a pinch of cayenne pepper, they're sweet and salty with just the right amount of heat. These cashews also make a great host gift, packed in a pretty glass jar. If you make them for a party, just note that they have a habit of mysteriously disappearing entirely before anyone arrives. You might just want to double the recipe.

1. Preheat the oven to 350°F and line a sheet pan with parchment paper.

2. Place the egg whites in a large bowl and whisk them vigorously until frothy, about 30 seconds. Add the brown sugar, honey, melted butter, salt, and cayenne and whisk until smooth. Add the cashews and toss well with a rubber spatula.

3. Transfer to the prepared pan, scraping the bowl with a spatula, and spread the cashews into a single layer. Bake for 20 to 25 minutes, tossing every 10 minutes, until the cashews are golden brown and the liquid on the pan has evaporated. The nuts will be sticky and will crisp up as they cool.

4. Sprinkle the cashews with flaky sea salt, then set aside until completely cool. Break the cashews apart if necessary and transfer to an airtight container. They will keep for up to 3 days, stored at room temperature.

COOKING FOR A CROWD
To make a double batch, use two sheet pans.

Beach Water

MAKES 8 DRINKS

Ice, for serving

1 (16-ounce) bottle
unsweetened coconut water,
such as Harmless Harvest
(see Tip)

½ cup vodka

¼ teaspoon kosher salt

Large handful of fresh mint
leaves (about ½ cup)

Fresh mint sprigs, for serving

When I moved to East Hampton right after college, I didn't know anyone who lived there year-round except for my friend Peyton's parents, Nancy and Chris. They had introduced me to Ina in the first place. Peyton, like most of my other friends from college, lived in New York City, and in his absence, his parents took me under their wing. They invited me to dinner, to the movies, and even included me in extended family gatherings. Nancy and I became especially close, and one day I realized she was more than just Peyton's mom. She'd become a real friend.

One summer day at the beach, I met Nancy's friend Anne, a cowboy hat–wearing media executive with an infectious laugh who loved to cook as much as I did. Anne was armed with a thermos of her signature "hydrating" beach cocktail—coconut water, mint, and a splash of vodka, with tons of ice—to share with friends who stopped by to chat.

While Nancy didn't cook much, she was the kind of person who was genuinely curious and enthusiastic about the things her friends loved—which included a lot of talk about recipes and cookbooks with Anne and me. Nancy's ability to engage and lift up the people around her was remarkable. She and Anne were some of my first cheerleaders when I began writing recipes, and I will be forever grateful for their support in those early days.

We lost Nancy a few years ago, far too soon. This recipe is for her, and it always reminds me of the golden afternoons we spent together on the beach.

1. Fill a glass pitcher with ice. Add the coconut water, vodka, and salt and stir.

2. Rub the mint leaves gently between your fingers to release the oils, then add them to the pitcher and stir.

3. Serve the cocktails in ice-filled tumblers (or a water bottle—wink, wink) with additional mint sprigs for garnish.

TIP

If you've bought bottled coconut water, you may have noticed that sometimes it's pale pink. That's because pure coconut water turns pink as its sugars oxidize. Rest assured, the pink color is completely natural and won't affect the flavor of this drink!

Brown Bread Crackers
with Crème Fraîche & Smoked Salmon

MAKES ABOUT 50 SMALL CRACKERS

For the Brown Bread Crackers

1 stick (4 ounces/113 grams) salted butter, at room temperature

2 tablespoons light or dark brown sugar

¼ teaspoon kosher salt

1½ cups (195 grams) whole wheat flour, plus more for rolling

¼ cup (60 grams) buttermilk, shaken

Flaky sea salt

For assembly

8 ounces crème fraîche

8 ounces thinly sliced smoked salmon, cut into 1-inch pieces

Freshly ground black pepper

Fresh dill sprigs, for serving

Lemon slices, for serving

TIP

The thinner you're able to roll the dough, the crisper the crackers will be. Use lots of flour when rolling, and keep the dough moving on the board as much as possible to avoid sticking. The crackers may seem slightly soft when they come out of the oven, but they'll crisp up as they cool!

Everyone always complains about the price of gas, but can we talk about the price of a decent box of crackers? Once you make homemade crackers, you may, like me, be extremely tempted to go into the cracker business.

These particular crackers are inspired by the many loaves of Irish brown bread I ate when I lived in Dublin, studying at Trinity College for a semester. Served in almost every Irish pub, this earthy whole wheat bread is so hearty it could be a meal in itself, slathered with salted Irish butter.

I loved the idea of a whole wheat cracker—made with Irish butter—that toed the line between sweet and savory. After a bit of experimenting, I came up with my perfect cracker: one inspired by the flavors of Irish brown bread, but with a texture all its own. Somewhere between a cracker and a savory shortbread cookie, these are delicious topped with crème fraîche and smoked salmon—another delight from the Emerald Isle!

1. **Make the brown bread crackers:** Preheat the oven to 375°F and line two sheet pans with parchment paper.

2. In a stand mixer fitted with the paddle attachment, combine the butter, brown sugar, and salt and beat on medium speed until creamy. Scrape the sides and bottom of the bowl. With the mixer on low, add half the flour and mix until just incorporated. Add the buttermilk and combine, then add the rest of the flour. Mix until the dough just comes together, scraping the sides of the bowl with a spatula if necessary.

3. Dump the dough out onto a generously floured board or cold countertop and shape into a rectangle. Roll the dough as thin as possible, no thicker than ⅛-inch (see Tip). Using a paring knife or a pizza cutter, cut the dough into 2-inch squares. (It's okay if they aren't perfect.) Reroll the scraps until you've used all the dough. Transfer the crackers to the prepared sheet pans, using a spatula if necessary, and spacing them ½-inch apart. Using a fork, prick each cracker in a few places. Sprinkle with flaky sea salt.

4. Bake the sheet pans, one at a time, until the crackers are lightly browned at the edges and on the bottom, 7 to 10 minutes. Cool completely on the pan.

5. **To assemble:** Spread 1 teaspoon crème fraîche on each cracker and top with a small piece of smoked salmon. Arrange the crackers on a serving platter, garnish with black pepper, dill, and lemon slices and serve immediately.

GET AHEAD

The crackers will keep for up to 3 days at room temperature, stored in a sealable plastic bag or other container.

Gin Martini with Rosemary & Grapefruit

MAKES 2 DRINKS

Ice, for serving

4 ounces (½ cup) chilled gin, such as Hendrick's

2 ounces (¼ cup) freshly squeezed grapefruit juice (1 grapefruit)

1 ounce (2 tablespoons) dry vermouth

2 grapefruit twists (see Tip), for serving

Small fresh rosemary sprigs, for serving

One of my favorite restaurants near us in the Hudson Valley is Stissing House in Pine Plains, New York. It's owned by Clare de Boer, who not only makes the most delicious rustic-yet-elevated tavern food, but also knows how to make a room seriously cozy. Sipping a martini in an armchair by one of the restaurant's many fireplaces is just about my favorite way to spend a cold winter night.

This recipe is a riff on Stissing House's "Pine Plains martini," a dry gin martini with a grapefruit twist and a spritz of pine needle essence. It's woodsy, citrusy, and always served in a beautifully frosted glass. My version has a splash of grapefruit juice for a touch of sweetness and a rosemary sprig to mimic the fragrant hint of pine.

1. Place two martini glasses in the freezer to chill while you make the drinks.

2. Fill a large cocktail shaker half full with ice. Add the gin, grapefruit juice, and vermouth and shake vigorously for 30 seconds. Strain into the two chilled glasses. Garnish each drink with a grapefruit peel. Rub a rosemary sprig around the rim of each glass, then drop the sprig into the drink. Serve immediately.

TIP

To make a grapefruit twist, use a vegetable peeler to remove a 3-inch-wide piece of grapefruit peel, avoiding the white pith. Hold the peel over the cocktail and bend it into a twisted shape, releasing the grapefruit's fragrant oils. This technique also works with lemon and orange peels, depending on the cocktail you're making.

Baked Crab Dip with Sweet Corn & Old Bay

SERVES 6

1 large or 2 small scallions, trimmed

½ tablespoon extra-virgin olive oil

½ cup fresh corn kernels (from 1 ear)

2 tablespoons minced jalapeño pepper (about half a medium jalapeño)

4 ounces cream cheese, at room temperature

⅓ cup plus 2 tablespoons grated Parmesan cheese, divided

3 tablespoons mayonnaise

1 tablespoon freshly squeezed lemon juice

½ teaspoon Old Bay seasoning, plus more for serving

½ teaspoon kosher salt

8 ounces fresh lump crabmeat

Sliced cucumbers, crackers, or pita, for serving

When it comes to party appetizers, I have a few guiding principles. First, they should be easy to make (especially when there is an entire dinner to cook!). Second, I want to be able to make them entirely or mostly in advance. Finally, and most important, they should be crowd-pleasers that set the tone for a delicious evening and make everyone feel welcome. This crab dip is a 3/3, slam dunk, home run.

Creamy baked dips are always a hit, and with fresh crab and corn kernels off the cob, this one feels especially luxurious. Luxurious *and* practical— you can assemble the whole thing in advance, pop it into the oven at the opportune moment, and pull it out when it's bubbling and browned on top. Serve the dip straight from the oven with lots of crackers and lightly salted cucumber slices for dipping.

1. Preheat the oven to 375°F.

2. Thinly slice the scallion, keeping the dark green parts separate from the light green and white parts. In an 8-inch skillet, heat the oil over medium heat. Add the corn, white and light green parts of the scallion, and jalapeño and cook, stirring occasionally, until the vegetables are tender, 3 to 5 minutes. Set aside to cool slightly.

3. In a medium bowl, combine the cream cheese, ⅓ cup of the Parmesan, the mayonnaise, lemon juice, ½ teaspoon of the Old Bay, and the salt and mix until smooth. Stir in the cooked corn/jalapeño mixture, then gently fold in the crabmeat.

4. Scrape the mixture into a shallow 1-quart baking dish and smooth into an even layer. Sprinkle the remaining 2 tablespoons Parmesan on top and sprinkle with more Old Bay.

5. Bake uncovered until bubbling and golden brown on top, about 25 minutes. Garnish with the dark green parts of the scallion, and set aside for 10 minutes to cool slightly. Serve hot with sliced cucumbers and crackers or pita.

COOKING FOR A CROWD
This recipe is a great one to double when you're having a larger gathering. You can bake it in a 2-quart baking dish, or two 1-quart baking dishes.

Garibaldi Spritz

2 cups freshly squeezed orange juice (about 8 oranges), strained to remove the pulp

½ cup Campari

2 cups sparkling water or Prosecco

Ice, for serving

8 orange slices, for serving

This drink comes with a history lesson: In the early 1800s, the Italian peninsula was not one unified country, but a land composed of many small, independent states. Giuseppe Garibaldi was one of the generals responsible for bringing the North and South together and establishing the nation of Italy. The Garibaldi Negroni is named for him, because it combines Campari from Northern Italy and orange juice from Southern Italy to make one harmonious drink.

This recipe is my take on a Garibaldi Spritz, lightened up with a splash of sparkling water or Prosecco in place of the gin or vodka. It's a refreshing, low-alcohol cocktail for *aperitivo* (Italian cocktail hour), but I also like to serve it in lieu of mimosas at brunch. With just a slight hint of bitterness from the Campari, it tastes like grown-up orange juice in the best way possible. Use Prosecco for a slightly sweeter, more festive drink, or sparkling water for a simpler, more refreshing one.

1. In a glass pitcher, combine the orange juice and Campari. Store, covered, in the refrigerator until you plan to serve the drinks (up to 8 hours).

2. Just before serving, add the sparkling water or Prosecco to the pitcher and stir. Divide the cocktail mixture among 8 ice-filled wineglasses or tumblers. Garnish each drink with an orange slice and serve immediately.

Cherry, Nectarine & Jalapeño Salsa

MAKES ABOUT 3 CUPS

2 yellow nectarines, pitted

2 cups sweet red cherries, pitted

¼ cup minced red onion

3 tablespoons minced, seeded jalapeño pepper (1 large)

1 tablespoon freshly squeezed lime juice

½ teaspoon kosher salt, plus more to taste

⅓ cup fresh basil or cilantro leaves

Tortilla chips, for serving

File this one under "recipes to make when it's too hot to cook." This fruity, spicy salsa is one of my favorite things to serve with drinks in the summer. It's easy to throw together and a surprising treat when people are expecting the same old jarred salsa and chips. It's also delicious on fish tacos or spooned over grilled steak.

If you've ever looked for perfectly ripe stone fruit (and let's be honest, squeezed every single peach in the store), you know that it can be like searching for a needle in a haystack. Thankfully, slightly underripe fruit is ideal for this recipe. Not only does the fruit keep its shape better when diced, but it's a little less sweet and doesn't overwhelm the other flavors in the salsa.

Serve with a big bowl of tortilla chips and cold beer.

1. Cut the nectarines and cherries into a small dice, somewhere between ¼ and ½ inch. Place them in a medium bowl and add the onion, jalapeños, lime juice, and salt and toss.

2. Just before serving, tear the basil leaves into small pieces, add them to the salsa, and toss. Add more salt to taste, and serve with tortilla chips. (This salsa can be stored in the refrigerator for up to 24 hours. Bring to room temperature and drain excess liquid before serving.)

TIP

Remove the jalapeño seeds and ribs for a mild salsa, or use the whole pepper for salsa with a serious kick.

Salads & a
Few Soups

Kale Salad with Gouda, Honeycrisp & Walnuts 50

Ratatouille Lentil Soup 53

Shaved Carrot Salad with Creamy Sesame-Ginger Dressing 54

Escarole Salad with Cara Cara Oranges,
Marcona Almonds & Goat Cheese 57

Taverna Salad 58

Marinated Fennel & Green Bean Salad 61

Sausage and White Bean Soup with Swiss Chard
& Skillet Croutons 06200

Little Gem Salad with Avocado Goddess Ranch Dressing
& Pickled Red Onions 65

Celery Waldorf with Pickled Golden Raisins 69

Melon & Cucumber Gazpacho 70

Arugula and Romaine Salad with Radish, Shaved Parm,
Pistachios & Mint 73

Avgolemono-ish Chicken Noodle Soup 74

Radicchio Salad with Pear, Cornbread
Crumbs & Bacon 77

Tomato and Peach Salad with Toasted Farro & Mozzarella 78

Kale Salad with Gouda, Honeycrisp & Walnuts

SERVES 4

1 cup walnuts

1 bunch curly kale (8 to 10 ounces)

¼ cup plus 1 teaspoon extra-virgin olive oil, divided

2 tablespoons cider vinegar

1 teaspoon maple syrup

½ teaspoon Dijon mustard

½ teaspoon kosher salt

Freshly ground black pepper

1 medium or half very large Honeycrisp apple, cored

¾ cup shaved aged Gouda cheese (about 2 ounces)

When I look back on my life thus far, I can separate it neatly into two eras: before kale and after kale. And while some people may yearn for ye old days of iceberg, I am personally very happy in this modern era of dark, leafy greens. Not only is kale nutrient- and fiber-packed, but it's got a great, hardy texture that holds up nicely when dressed. No wilting leaves here!

This kale salad is one I make all the time in the fall and winter. It's got lots of crunch, thanks to Honeycrisp apples and walnuts, and slivers of creamy Gouda cheese in every bite. If you haven't tried aged Gouda, you're in for a treat—it's rich and nutty, almost like an aged cheddar crossed with Parmesan. It's an especially nice complement to the crisp, sweet apples and cider vinaigrette in this salad.

1. Preheat the oven to 350°F.

2. Place the walnuts on a sheet pan and toast in the oven for 10 minutes. Cool, then coarsely chop and set aside.

3. Wash the kale leaves and pat them dry with a clean kitchen towel. Lay the leaves flat on a cutting board and cut down both sides of the center rib, discarding the rib. Chop the leaves and place them in a large bowl. Drizzle the kale with 1 teaspoon of the olive oil and massage it into the leaves for 30 seconds, to tenderize them.

4. In a glass measuring cup, combine the vinegar, maple syrup, mustard, salt, and a few grinds of black pepper. Add the remaining ¼ cup olive oil and whisk vigorously until smooth. Pour the dressing over the kale and toss well.

5. Thinly slice the apple, then stack and cut the slices in half crosswise. Add the apples to the salad, along with the walnuts and the Gouda. Toss well and serve.

MAKE IT A MEAL

If you want to bulk up this salad for an easy weeknight dinner, as we often do, add some shredded rotisserie chicken or canned chickpeas.

Ratatouille Lentil Soup

MAKES 3 QUARTS/
SERVES 6 TO 8

5 tablespoons extra-virgin olive oil, divided, plus more as needed

1 pound eggplant, unpeeled and ½-inch diced (1 medium eggplant)

1 large yellow onion, chopped (2 cups)

1 pound zucchini, ½-inch diced (2 medium zucchini)

2 tablespoons minced garlic (4 large cloves)

1 teaspoon dried oregano

2 tablespoons tomato paste

8 cups (2 quarts) low-sodium vegetable broth

1 (14.5-ounce) can crushed tomatoes

1 cup French green lentils, rinsed

1 cup jarred roasted red peppers, drained and chopped

2 teaspoons kosher salt, plus more to taste

½ teaspoon freshly ground black pepper, plus more to taste

½ cup fresh basil leaves, plus more for serving

1 tablespoon balsamic vinegar

This rustic lentil soup is inspired by the flavors of ratatouille, the beloved Provençal dish of stewed summer vegetables and herbs. Lentil soup is a hearty, comforting soup, and all the different veggies—zucchini, eggplant, roasted red peppers, and tomatoes—give this one lots of color and texture. A final splash of balsamic vinegar and a handful of torn basil leaves makes this soup taste like a summer treat on a cold winter's day.

1. In a large pot, heat 3 tablespoons of the olive oil over medium-high heat. Add the eggplant and cook, tossing occasionally, until lightly browned and starting to soften, about 5 minutes. Add a splash of oil if the eggplant begins to stick at any point.

2. Add the onion and zucchini to the pot, along with the remaining 2 tablespoons olive oil. Reduce the heat to medium and cook until the onion is tender and the zucchini is crisp-tender, 6 to 8 minutes. Add the garlic and oregano and cook for 30 seconds until fragrant.

3. Stir in the tomato paste and cook until it begins to darken in color, about 2 minutes. Add the vegetable broth, crushed tomatoes, lentils, roasted red peppers, salt, and black pepper and bring to a boil. Reduce the heat and simmer uncovered, stirring occasionally, until the lentils are tender, 50 minutes to 1 hour.

4. Off the heat, add the basil and vinegar and stir until the basil has wilted. Taste for seasonings and serve hot with a drizzle of olive oil, a few more basil leaves, and a sprinkle of salt and pepper.

Shaved Carrot Salad
with Creamy Sesame-Ginger Dressing

SERVES 4 TO 6

3 tablespoons tahini

3 tablespoons extra-virgin olive oil

3 tablespoons seasoned rice vinegar

2 teaspoons grated fresh ginger

1 teaspoon soy sauce

1 small garlic clove, grated on a Microplane

½ teaspoon kosher salt

1 tablespoon cold water

1½ pounds carrots, trimmed and peeled

½ cup thinly sliced scallions (2 to 3 scallions)

1 teaspoon sesame seeds

While I could eat this creamy sesame-ginger dressing on just about anything (rice noodles, grilled chicken, and steamed broccoli, to name a few), the magic of this salad is really the combination of tender shaved carrots and crunchy carrot matchsticks. The contrasting textures make for an incredibly satisfying salad that soaks up every bit of the creamy dressing. I like to serve it in the summer as a picnic side, and in the winter when I'm craving something fresh and crunchy.

1. In a medium bowl, whisk together the tahini, olive oil, vinegar, ginger, soy sauce, garlic, and salt. Add the cold water and whisk until smooth and creamy. Set aside.

2. Using a mandoline or a vegetable peeler, shave the carrots into long ribbons and place in a large bowl. (If you're using a vegetable peeler, hold each carrot flat against your cutting board with one hand and peel with the other.) Chop any leftover carrot pieces into matchsticks and add to the bowl, along with the scallions.

3. Pour the dressing over the salad and toss well with tongs. Sprinkle with sesame seeds and serve.

MAKE IT A MEAL
For a light weekday lunch or dinner, add some sautéed shrimp or Seared Salmon Fillets (page 262).

Escarole Salad with Cara Cara Oranges, Marcona Almonds & Goat Cheese

SERVES 4 TO 6

1 large head escarole (14 to 16 ounces)

¼ cup extra-virgin olive oil

1 tablespoon sherry vinegar

1 tablespoon honey

½ teaspoon Dijon mustard

Kosher salt and freshly ground black pepper

1 tablespoon minced shallots

2 Cara Cara or small navel oranges

½ cup Marcona almonds, coarsely chopped

2 ounces creamy goat cheese, crumbled

I'd always thought of escarole as a green that needed to be cooked until I had the escarole salad at Rucola, a neighborhood Italian restaurant we frequented during our year-and-a-half stint in Brooklyn. The salad has a wildflower honey vinaigrette, crunchy Marcona almonds, and a creamy smoked feta that melts into the dressing as the greens get tossed. The escarole leaves soften just enough to be tender and delicious without wilting. Salad perfection.

This recipe is my little homage Rucola's salad. I've swapped in creamy goat cheese for the soft feta, because it's easier to find, and I've added some sliced oranges for a little burst of citrus. I love the bright coral color of Cara Caras, but any orange on the smaller side will work!

1. Remove and discard the outer, dark green leaves from the escarole. Separate the rest of the leaves and wash and dry them thoroughly in a salad spinner or with a kitchen towel. Tear the leaves into bite-size pieces and place in a large bowl.

2. In a small liquid measuring cup or bowl, whisk together the olive oil, vinegar, honey, mustard, ½ teaspoon salt, and a few grinds of black pepper. Stir in the shallots and set aside.

3. Using a small serrated knife, peel the oranges and trim to remove any remaining pith. Slice them crosswise into thin rounds and remove the seeds.

4. Pour the dressing over the escarole and toss well. Add the almonds, goat cheese, and oranges and toss gently. Seasons with salt and pepper and serve.

SIMPLE SWAP

The Marcona almonds make this salad extra special, but you could also use regular almonds, toasted walnuts, or shelled pistachios.

MAKE IT A MEAL

Adding a cup of cooked farro, quinoa, or wheatberries would be a delicious way to bulk up this salad.

Taverna Salad

SERVES 4 TO 6

⅓ cup extra-virgin olive oil, plus more for drizzling

2 tablespoons red wine vinegar

1 teaspoon minced garlic (1 small clove)

½ teaspoon dried oregano

Kosher salt and freshly ground black pepper

3 medium tomatoes, cored, seeded, and ½-inch diced, or 1 cup halved cherry tomatoes

1 (15-ounce) can chickpeas, drained and rinsed

1 orange or yellow bell pepper, cored and ½-inch diced

Half a large English cucumber, halved, seeded, and ½-inch diced (about 1½ cups)

½ cup pitted Kalamata olives

¼ cup chopped fresh parsley

¼ cup minced red onion or shallot

2 tablespoons capers, drained and coarsely chopped

2 scallions, thinly sliced

1 (6-inch) pita

1 (8-ounce) block Halloumi cheese, patted dry and cut into ¾-inch-thick slices

This is my husband Joe's favorite salad. Notice it does not contain any lettuce—this is not a coincidence! Kidding aside, we both love this crunchy, colorful meal of a salad, and one or the other of us makes it a few times a month. It's inspired by two of my all-time favorite salads: horiatiki, the classic Greek salad, and fattoush, the Lebanese salad of vegetables and pieces of fried pita. I like to add pan-fried Halloumi to make this feel more like dinner, but a 6-ounce block of feta works great, too, if you can't find Halloumi or want to skip a step.

1. In a small bowl, combine the olive oil, vinegar, garlic, oregano, ½ teaspoon salt, and a few grinds of black pepper, and whisk vigorously.

2. In a large bowl, combine the tomatoes, chickpeas, bell pepper, cucumber, olives, parsley, red onion, capers, and scallions. Pour the dressing over the salad and toss well.

3. Chop the pita into 1-inch pieces and place them in a small bowl. Drizzle with olive oil, sprinkle with salt, and toss to coat. Heat an 8-inch skillet over medium heat. Add the pita and cook, tossing often, until toasted and golden brown, about 5 minutes. Return to the small bowl to cool, reserving the skillet.

4. Place the Halloumi slices on a small plate and drizzle with olive oil. Heat the same skillet over medium-high heat, add the slices of Halloumi, and cook until golden brown, 2 to 3 minutes per side. Transfer to a cutting board and cut the slices into bite-size cubes.

5. Add the pita and Halloumi to the salad, toss well, and serve.

GET AHEAD

You can do all the prep and chopping in advance and just toast the pita and Halloumi before serving. To save time, you can add a large handful crumbled pita chips instead of making your own.

LEFTOVERS FOR LUNCH

This salad keeps well overnight, and I often double the recipe to have leftovers for lunch the next day.

Marinated Fennel & Green Bean Salad

SERVES 6

Kosher salt and freshly ground black pepper

1 pound haricots verts or string beans, trimmed

⅓ cup extra-virgin olive oil

Grated zest of half an orange

2 tablespoons freshly squeezed orange juice

Grated zest of half a lemon

1 tablespoon freshly squeezed lemon juice

½ teaspoon Dijon mustard

½ cup thinly sliced shallot (1 large shallot)

1 medium fennel bulb, cored and thinly sliced crosswise (about 8 ounces)

½ cup pitted Kalamata olives

Chopped fennel fronds or fresh parsley, for serving

Good food has a magical ability to transport you to another time in your life, or another part of the world, without leaving the comfort of your own kitchen. This chic, summery salad, with its wild tangle of fennel, green beans, and herbs, immediately takes me from my own backyard to the South of France, or maybe the Italian Islands. I like to serve it with a glass of chilled rosé or dry white wine and some nice crusty bread to complete the journey.

1. Bring a large pot of salted water to a boil, and fill a large bowl with ice water. Add the beans to the boiling water and cook until just tender, 3 to 5 minutes. (Haricots verts will cook more quickly than string beans.) Using tongs, immediately transfer the beans to the ice water to cool, then place in a colander to drain.

2. In a large bowl, combine the olive oil, orange zest, orange juice, lemon zest, lemon juice, mustard, ½ teaspoon salt, and ¼ teaspoon pepper. Whisk vigorously, then add the shallot and whisk again.

3. Pat the green beans dry with a kitchen towel or paper towel and add them to the bowl, along with the fennel and olives. Toss well. Set the salad aside to marinate for at least 1 hour at room temperature, tossing occasionally, or for up to 6 hours in the refrigerator. (Allow the salad to come to room temperature for 1 hour before serving.)

4. Spoon the salad onto a flat serving platter, including any dressing that's left in the bowl. Sprinkle generously with salt and black pepper, and garnish with fennel fronds or chopped parsley. Serve at room temperature.

MAKE IT A MEAL
To make this salad into a light meal, add a piece of roasted or grilled salmon, or any fish, really.

GET AHEAD
This is an ideal salad to serve when you're having company, because you can make the whole dish in advance and let it marinate at room temperature until you're ready to eat.

Sausage and White Bean Soup with Swiss Chard & Skillet Croutons

SERVES 6

1 bunch Swiss chard (about 8 ounces)

5 tablespoons extra-virgin olive oil, divided

1 pound hot Italian sausage, casings removed

1 large yellow onion, chopped

4 garlic cloves, minced

½ cup dry white wine

1 (15-ounce) can cannellini beans, drained and rinsed

4 cups (32 ounces) low-sodium chicken broth

Kosher salt and freshly ground black pepper

3 cups ¾-inch cubed bread (about 4.5 ounces)

Lots of freshly grated Parmesan cheese, for serving

This soup's magic is its all-around speediness. While some soups require an hour or two of simmering, this one delivers deep, satisfying flavor in just 30 minutes. Thirty minutes! The canned beans are definitely a time-saver, but the MVP here is really the Italian sausage—it lends depth to the broth and gives the soup an unbeatable savory richness. While you can use any sturdy green, I love the pop of color the Swiss chard stems add. They're the perfect fresh, earthy note in this otherwise hearty soup.

1. Rinse the Swiss chard under cold, running water. Separate the leaves from the center stems. Discard any stems thicker than ½ inch, then slice the remaining stems into ½-inch pieces and set them aside.

2. Line a large plate with paper towels. In a 10-inch Dutch oven, heat 1 tablespoon of the olive oil over medium-high heat. Add the sausage and cook, breaking up the meat with a wooden spoon, until browned, 4 to 6 minutes. Using a slotted spoon, transfer the sausage to the paper towels to drain and set aside.

3. Reduce the heat to medium and add 1 tablespoon of the olive oil. Add the onion and chard stems and cook, stirring occasionally, until tender, 6 to 8 minutes. Add the garlic and cook for 1 more minute, until fragrant. Add the wine and cook, scraping the bottom of the pan, until most of the liquid has evaporated.

4. Add the white beans, the cooked sausage, the chicken broth, and 1 teaspoon salt. Bring to a boil, then reduce the heat and simmer for 10 minutes, stirring occasionally.

5. Meanwhile, make the croutons: In a large skillet, heat the remaining 3 table-spoons olive oil over medium heat. Add the bread cubes in a single layer and cook, tossing often, until browned all over, 3 to 5 minutes. Sprinkle with salt and transfer to a plate to cool.

6. Taste the soup and season with salt and pepper as needed. Serve hot in shallow bowls, topped with croutons and a small mountain of freshly grated Parmesan cheese.

Little Gem Salad with Avocado Goddess Dressing & Pickled Red Onions

SERVES 4

1 teaspoon chopped garlic
(1 medium clove)

3 tablespoons chopped
fresh dill

2 tablespoons minced fresh
chives or scallions (white and
green parts)

1 Hass avocado (6 to 8 ounces),
halved and pitted

½ cup mayonnaise

3 tablespoons freshly
squeezed lemon juice (1 large
lemon)

Kosher salt and freshly ground
black pepper

12 ounces Little Gem lettuce or
romaine leaves, torn if large

½ cup Quick-Pickled Red
Onion (recipe follows)

This vibrant salad is fun to make, and it's great for a gathering. With crunchy lettuce, bright green dressing, and vinegary pickled onions, it's inviting and a little funky—just how I like my parties! The avocado goddess dressing is herby, lemony, creamy—and happens to be completely dairy-free. It also makes a delicious dip for veggies, or a tangy, creamy spread for turkey sandwiches.

1.   In a food processor, combine the garlic, dill, and chives and process until finely chopped. Scoop the avocado into the processor and add the mayonnaise, lemon juice, 1 teaspoon salt, and a few grinds of black pepper. Process until smooth, 10 to 15 seconds. Set aside. (Or store in a sealed container in the refrigerator for up to 2 days before using.)

2.   Wash and dry the lettuce leaves in a salad spinner. Place the lettuce in a very large bowl and drizzle about half the dressing over the salad. Add the pickled onions and toss until well mixed. Add more dressing to taste, season with a pinch of salt and black pepper, and serve.

SIMPLE SWAP
While Little Gem lettuce has been on restaurant menus for years, I'm just now seeing it at my local grocery stores. If you're having trouble finding it where you live, feel free to use romaine instead. It's really the crunch you're going for.

RECIPE CONTINUES

QUICK-PICKLED RED ONION

Makes about 1½ cups

1½ cups packed thinly sliced red onion (1 medium onion)

½ cup red wine vinegar

1 tablespoon granulated sugar

1 teaspoon kosher salt

1.   Place the onion in a half-pint jar or other heatproof container and pack lightly with a spoon.

2.   In a small saucepan or skillet, combine the vinegar, ¼ cup water, the sugar, and salt. Bring to a simmer, stir to dissolve the sugar, then carefully pour the mixture over the onion.

3.   Set aside until cool. Use immediately or refrigerate for up to 5 days before serving.

Celery Waldorf with Pickled Golden Raisins

SERVES 6

½ cup golden raisins

4 tablespoons white wine vinegar or champagne vinegar, divided

1 tablespoon unsalted butter

2 tablespoons maple syrup

1 cup walnuts, coarsely chopped

Kosher salt and freshly ground black pepper

1 large bunch celery (about 1¾ pounds)

1 large Honeycrisp or Fuji apple

¼ cup chopped fresh parsley

5 tablespoons extra-virgin olive oil

1 cup crumbled creamy blue cheese, such as Bleu d'Auvergne or Gorgonzola (4 ounces)

The Waldorf Salad was first served at New York City's Waldorf-Astoria Hotel in the 1890s, and it's endured as an American classic. It's changed with the tastes over the years, but even a pit stop in the land of 1950s Jell-O and mini marshmallows hasn't dampened the appeal of this crunchy, colorful salad.

Celery never gets much attention in a Waldorf (or in most dishes for that matter), but I think its mild, herby flavor and supreme crunchiness makes it an ideal base for a salad. Here, thinly sliced celery is joined by the other classic Waldorf ingredients—walnuts, apples, and crumbled blue cheese—with pickled raisins for a vinegary tang and contrast in texture.

There's something holiday-ish to me about this combination of flavors, and it's a playfully retro salad to serve alongside classic wintry dishes like roast chicken or short ribs. Any blue cheese will work, but I like to choose one that's semi-firm so it crumbles nicely.

1. In a small skillet, combine the raisins and 2 tablespoons of the vinegar. Bring to a simmer over medium heat and cook until the vinegar has almost completely evaporated, about 2 minutes. Transfer the raisins and any remaining vinegar to a small bowl and set aside to cool.

2. Have a piece of parchment paper at the ready. Rinse and dry the skillet and return it to the stove over medium-low heat. Add the butter and maple syrup and swirl the pan until the butter has melted. Add the walnuts and cook, tossing often, until the pan is dry, 3 to 5 minutes. Working quickly, transfer the walnuts to the parchment, spreading them out as much as possible. Sprinkle with a little salt, then set aside to cool.

3. Trim the celery ribs, setting aside the leaves. Thinly slice the celery on the diagonal and place it in a large bowl. Halve, core, and thinly slice the apple, then cut the slices in half crosswise and add them to the bowl, along with the parsley and celery leaves. (Tear any large celery leaves in half.)

4. In a small bowl or glass measuring cup, combine the olive oil, the remaining 2 tablespoons vinegar, ¼ teaspoon salt, and a few grinds of black pepper and whisk vigorously until emulsified. Pour about three-quarters of the dressing over the celery and apples and toss well.

5. Add the cooled raisins and walnuts and the blue cheese to the bowl. Toss gently. Drizzle the remaining dressing over the salad, and serve at room temperature.

Melon & Cucumber Gazpacho

SERVES 4 TO 6

1 large English cucumber
(about 14 ounces)

4 cups diced cantaloupe or
honeydew melon (about half a
4-pound melon)

1 cup orange or yellow cherry
tomatoes

2 tablespoons chopped
seeded jalapeño pepper
(about 1 small jalapeño)

¼ cup chopped red onion

2 tablespoons freshly
squeezed lime juice (1 to
2 limes)

2 tablespoons white wine
vinegar

1½ teaspoons kosher salt

¼ cup extra-virgin olive oil,
plus more for drizzling

Fresh mint, basil, or cilantro,
for serving

There's a saying, "Things that grow together go together." This is not a hard and fast rule, but it is something I like to keep in mind when I'm dreaming up new recipe ideas. With the exception of the lime, all the fresh ingredients in this gazpacho grow in the summer, making this recipe a "one-stopper" at the farmers' market.

Paired with savory ingredients like tomatoes, peppers, and red onion, melon is sweet, mellow, and refreshing. You can make this recipe with cantaloupe or honeydew, but the melon is the dominant flavor here, so the ripest melon you can find will give you the most delicious, stand-out flavor. (Look for melons that are fragrant and feel heavy for their size.)

This soup makes a perfect first course in the blazing heat of summer, garnished with whatever herbs you have on hand and a generous swirl of olive oil. I like to serve it in small bowls or in glasses as a perfect, refreshing start to a summer meal.

1. Peel the cucumber, cut halve it lengthwise, and using a small spoon, scoop out the seeds. Coarsely chop the cucumber and place it in a blender, along with the melon, tomatoes, jalapeño, red onion, lime juice, vinegar, and salt. (If your blender can't fit everything at once, you can blend in two batches, combining everything together at the end.)

2. Blend on high, until the vegetables are coarsely blended, but still have some texture. Add the olive oil and blend on high for 10 more seconds, until smooth. (If you're using a powerful blender, such as Vitamix, blend on a lower speed.)

3. Transfer the soup to a glass pitcher or storage container and refrigerate for at least 2 hours, or overnight.

4. Stir, then serve cold in small bowls or glasses, topped with a drizzle of oil and a few fresh basil, mint, or cilantro leaves.

MAKE IT A MEAL
Top with grilled or sautéed shrimp and serve with toasted crostini for a light summer lunch or dinner.

COOKING FOR A CROWD
You can strecth this recipe to serve up to 12 people if you serve it as an hors d'ouevre in small decorative glasses or "shooters."

Arugula and Romaine Salad
with Radish, Shaved Parm, Pistachios & Mint

SERVES 6 TO 8

4 cups baby arugula (about half a 5-ounce box)

1 romaine heart, trimmed and sliced crosswise into ½-inch-wide ribbons

1 bunch radishes (about 6 radishes), trimmed and washed

½ cup salted roasted pistachios, coarsely chopped

1 cup shaved pecorino or Parmesan cheese (3 ounces)

2 tablespoons freshly squeezed lemon juice

½ teaspoon kosher salt

Freshly ground black pepper

⅓ cup extra-virgin olive oil

¾ cup fresh mint leaves (1 bunch)

Of all the salads in this book, this is the one I make most often. It has lots of color, crunch, and a zingy lemon dressing. The pistachios and shaved Parmesan make it feel a little bit luxurious but still fresh and light. I used to think of this recipe as a spring salad, but the truth is, I make it all year long, and especially love it in the winter to brighten up a hearty main course. If you're feeling brave you can use a mandoline to thinly slice the radishes, but a sharp knife and a little bit of patience will do the trick just fine.

1. In a large shallow bowl, combine the arugula and romaine. Using a mandoline or a sharp knife, carefully slice the radishes paper-thin, then add them to the bowl, along with the pistachios and cheese.

2. In a small bowl or glass measuring up, combine the lemon juice, salt, and a few grinds of black pepper, then slowly whisk in the olive oil.

3. Just before serving, pour the dressing over the salad and toss well. Tear the mint leaves into pieces, scatter them on the salad, and toss again. Serve immediately.

MAKE IT A MEAL
Add a simply cooked piece of salmon, some shredded chicken, or canned chickpeas to make this salad into a super-fresh and satisfying dinner.

Avgolemono-ish Chicken Noodle Soup

SERVES 8 TO 10

2 bone-in, skin-on chicken breasts (about 12 ounces each)

3 tablespoons extra-virgin olive oil, plus more for drizzling

Kosher salt and freshly ground black pepper

1½ cups small-diced carrots (about 3 medium carrots)

1½ cups small-diced celery (about 3 large celery ribs)

1 large yellow onion, chopped

12 cups (3 quarts) low-sodium chicken broth

1 cup ditalini, acini di pepe, or pearl couscous

1 (15-ounce) can chickpeas, rinsed and drained

3 large egg yolks

⅓ cup freshly squeezed lemon juice (2 lemons)

3 cups baby spinach

¼ cup minced fresh dill or parsley, plus more for serving

This cozy chicken soup is a regular in my winter rotation, and a great one to make for a friend or family member who's under the weather. It's inspired by Greek avgolemono, in which egg yolks and lemon juice are whisked into the broth just before serving. (Translated literally, avgolemono means "egg," *avgo*, "lemon," *lemono*.) The egg yolks add a subtle, savory richness to the broth, without tasting "eggy," and a splash of lemon juice brightens up the whole bowl.

This is my sister-in-law Julie's favorite soup. She can't eat dairy, and it delivers on the richness of a cream-based soup without a drop of milk.

1. Preheat the oven to 350°F and line a sheet pan with parchment paper.

2. Pat the chicken breasts dry and place them on the prepared pan. Drizzle some olive oil over the breasts, sprinkle with ½ teaspoon salt and a few grinds of black pepper.

3. Transfer to the oven and roast until just cooked through, 30 to 35 minutes. Set aside until cool enough to handle, then shred the cooled chicken breasts into bite-size pieces, discarding the skin and bones.

4. Meanwhile, in a large pot, heat the olive oil over medium heat. Add the carrots, celery, and onion and cook, stirring occasionally, until the onion is translucent and the vegetables are beginning to soften, 8 to 10 minutes.

5. Add the broth, 1 tablespoon salt, and 1 teaspoon pepper and bring to a boil over medium-high heat. Reduce the heat and cook at a vigorous simmer until the broth has reduced slightly and the vegetables are tender, about 10 minutes.

6. Add the pasta and chickpeas and cook, stirring occasionally, until the pasta is al dente. Reduce the heat to low, add the chicken and cook until just heated through. Set the soup aside off the heat.

7. In a medium bowl, whisk together the egg yolks and lemon juice. Whisking constantly, slowly pour a ladleful of hot broth into the egg mixture. Repeat several more times until the mixture is warm to the touch. Stirring constantly, gradually pour the egg mixture into the soup.

8. Add the spinach and dill and stir until the spinach wilts. Taste for seasonings, then serve hot, garnishing each serving with extra dill and a few grinds of black pepper.

SIMPLE SWAP
This soup can easily be made gluten-free by substituting cooked white or brown rice for the pasta or couscous.

Radicchio Salad
with Pear, Cornbread Crumbs & Bacon

SERVES 4 TO 6

2 cups coarsely crumbled cornbread (see page 258) or bakery corn muffin (about 4½ ounces)

⅓ cup plus 1 tablespoon extra-virgin olive oil, divided

Kosher salt and freshly ground black pepper

8 ounces sliced, thick-cut bacon

1 large (10-ounce) head radicchio, leaves separated

2 tablespoons red wine vinegar

1 tablespoon minced shallot

1 teaspoon whole-grain mustard

1 teaspoon honey

1 firm, ripe Anjou or other green pear, cored and cut into ¼-inch-thick slices

We all know someone who doesn't like bitter salad greens. You might even be that person. If so, don't stop reading! I think this salad just might convince you bitterness can actually be a good thing paired with the right dressing, and a complement to both savory and sweet toppings. (If bacon and cornbread crumbs can't convince you, I don't know what can!) This is a fun, colorful salad to serve alongside a hearty bowl of chili or soup, and it also makes a terrific lunch on its own.

1. Preheat the oven to 400°F.

2. Place the cornbread crumbs on a sheet pan, drizzle with 1 tablespoon of the olive oil, and sprinkle with ¼ teaspoon salt. Toss well and bake until lightly browned, 10 to 15 minutes, tossing once halfway through. Set aside until cool, then transfer the crumbs to a plate. Leave the oven on.

3. Wipe the sheet pan to remove any leftover crumbs and line it with foil. Arrange the bacon slices on the pan and bake until browned and crisp, 20 to 25 minutes. Transfer to a paper towel–lined plate to cool, then chop into ¾-inch pieces.

4. Meanwhile, rinse and dry the radicchio leaves. Tear the larger leaves into bite-size pieces, then place the radicchio in a large bowl.

5. In a large glass measuring cup, whisk together the vinegar, shallot, mustard, honey, ¼ teaspoon salt, and a few grinds of black pepper. Add the remaining ⅓ cup olive oil and whisk vigorously, until smooth.

6. Pour the dressing over the radicchio and toss gently with tongs or clean hands. Add the cornbread, bacon, and pear and toss gently until combined. Serve at room temperature.

GET AHEAD

You can prep the cornbread crumbs, bacon, and dressing ahead of time, and then combine everything before serving. Just be sure to hide the cooked bacon in the back of the fridge so it doesn't mysteriously disappear.

Tomato and Peach Salad
with Toasted Farro & Mozzarella

SERVES 4

Kosher salt and freshly
ground black pepper

½ cup pearled farro, rinsed

4 tablespoons extra-virgin
olive oil, divided

1 pint cherry tomatoes, halved
through the stem

2 peaches or nectarines, pitted
and cut into ½-inch wedges

4 ounces fresh mozzarella
cheese, torn into large shreds
(about ¾ cup)

1 tablespoon champagne
vinegar or white wine vinegar

¼ cup fresh mint or basil
leaves, chopped

It's tough to beat a simple salad of summer tomatoes and fresh mozzarella, but when you feel like a twist on that classic combo, give this recipe a try. Juicy peaches are a delicious complement to tomatoes (after all, they're both technically fruit!), and the crispy toasted farro adds a nice crunch, almost like tiny croutons on the salad. I toast cooked farro grains in the oven, until they're golden brown and slightly chewy. They add enough "oomph" to bump this salad into the lunch category—if you need my permission to eat a ball of mozzarella for lunch!

1.   Fill a medium saucepan with water and bring to a boil over high heat. Add 1 tablespoon salt and the farro. Reduce the heat to medium and simmer, uncovered, until the farro is tender, about 30 minutes.

2.   Meanwhile, preheat the oven to 375°F.

3.   When the farro is cooked, drain it thoroughly in a colander, then immediately transfer it to a sheet pan, spreading it out with a wooden spoon. Cool completely, then drizzle the farro with 1 tablespoon of the olive oil and ¼ teaspoon salt, and toss well. Spread the farro back out into an even layer, then toast in the oven until the grains begin to look toasted at the edges, 15 to 20 minutes, tossing once halfway through. Set aside to cool.

4.   Spread half of the farro on a large flat platter. Arrange the tomatoes, peaches, and mozzarella on top. In a large glass measuring cup, whisk together the remaining 3 tablespoons olive oil, the vinegar, and ¼ teaspoon salt. Drizzle the dressing evenly over the salad, then top with the remaining farro and the mint. Sprinkle lightly with salt and black pepper and serve at room temperature.

Chicken, Beef & Pork

One-Pan Chicken Meatballs with Red Sauce & Spinach

SERVES 4

½ cup panko (Japanese bread crumbs)

⅓ cup whole milk

2 garlic cloves, grated on a Microplane

1 pound ground dark meat chicken (not 100% breast meat)

1 large egg, lightly beaten

⅔ cup grated Parmesan cheese, divided

3 tablespoons chopped fresh parsley

½ teaspoon dried oregano

Extra-virgin olive oil

Kosher salt and freshly ground black pepper

1 (24-ounce) jar good-quality marinara or arrabbiata sauce, such as Rao's

1 (5-ounce) container baby spinach

Handful of fresh basil leaves, torn into pieces (optional)

Cooked pasta, crusty bread, or Creamy Polenta (page 162), for serving

You know you have a good recipe on your hands when grown-ups *and* kids like it. Such is the case with these simple chicken meatballs, which my friend Maggie's five-year-old son, Henry, requests on the regular. It may be tempting to bake these, but because chicken meatballs are so lean, pan-frying them is the key to developing lots of flavor and a nice crust. My favorite way to cook these meatballs is to brown them in a skillet and then simmer them in marinara sauce with lots of spinach stirred in, as I do here. Henry prefers them plain over buttered noodles, or as a snack in his lunchbox. If you want to go that route, cook the meatballs all the way through in the skillet, lowering the heat as necessary to prevent them from getting too dark on the outside.

1. In a small bowl, combine the panko, milk, and garlic and toss with a fork. Set aside.

2. In a large bowl, combine the chicken, egg, ⅓ cup of the Parmesan, the parsley, the oregano, 1 tablespoon olive oil, 1½ teaspoons salt, and ½ teaspoon black pepper. Mix gently but thoroughly with clean hands, or using two forks. Add the panko mixture and mix gently until just combined.

3. Pour a few tablespoons of olive oil into a small bowl. Coat your hands with oil, then form meatballs that are about 1¾ inches in diameter, dipping your fingers in the olive oil as necessary to prevent sticking. You should have about 16 meatballs.

4. Line a large plate with paper towels. In a 10-inch Dutch oven, heat 3 tablespoons olive oil over medium heat. Add about one third of the meatballs and cook, turning occasionally, until browned on all sides, about 4 minutes. Transfer to the paper towels and repeat with the remaining meatballs. You may need to reduce the heat slightly if the meatballs begin browning too quickly.

5. Return the browned meatballs to the pot and add the marinara sauce and ¼ cup water. Bring to a boil, then reduce the heat, partially cover, and simmer until the meatballs are cooked through and the sauce has reduced slightly, 10 to 15 minutes.

6. Stir in the spinach and cook until just wilted. Off the heat, stir in the remaining ⅓ cup Parmesan and the basil leaves, if using.

7. Serve hot with cooked pasta, crusty bread, or over polenta.

Cider-Glazed Sausages with Caramelized Apples & Fennel

SERVES 4

1 medium Honeycrisp or Fuji apple

3 tablespoons extra-virgin olive oil, divided

1 cup thinly sliced fennel (about half a medium bulb)

1 cup thinly sliced red onion (about half a large onion)

1 tablespoon maple syrup

4 tablespoons apple cider vinegar, divided

Kosher salt and freshly ground black pepper

4 sweet Italian sausage links (about 1 pound)

¾ cup fresh apple cider

Chopped fresh parsley or fennel fronds, for serving

I use Italian sausage often. It's flavorful, inexpensive, and cooks quickly, making it ideal for all kinds of weeknight dinners. In this one-pot recipe, the juices from the sausages simmer together with apple cider, caramelized red onion, and fennel to create a delicious and fragrant glaze. If you don't like fennel, you can double the onion or add some thinly sliced celery or Brussels sprouts in its place.

1. Core and thinly slice the apple, then stack the slices and cut them into thirds crosswise.

2. In a 10-inch Dutch oven or deep cast-iron skillet, heat 2 tablespoons of the olive oil over medium-low heat. Add the fennel, onion, apple, and maple syrup and cook, stirring occasionally, until lightly caramelized, about 15 minutes. (If the vegetables start browning too quickly, reduce the heat to low.)

3. Add 2 tablespoons of the vinegar and ½ teaspoon salt and stir, scraping up any browned bits from the pan. Transfer the mixture to a small bowl and carefully wipe out the pan with a paper towel.

4. Add the remaining 1 tablespoon olive oil to the pan and increase the heat to medium-high. When the oil is hot, add the sausages and cook, turning occasionally, until browned all over, 4 to 6 minutes. Reduce the heat to medium-low and add the cider (careful, it may splatter!). Simmer until the sausages are cooked through and the cider has reduced and thickened, 6 to 10 minutes, flipping the sausages once or twice. (If the sausages are cooked through before the cider has reduced, remove them from the pot while the cider finishes.)

5. Return the apples, fennel, and onion to the pan, along with the remaining 2 tablespoons vinegar. Toss to coat them with the sauce and spoon over the sausages. Season to taste with salt and pepper, sprinkle with parsley, and serve right from the pan.

MAKE IT A MEAL
Serve the sausages straight from the pot with crusty bread, a Simple Green Salad (page 263), and a lightly chilled red wine.

Champagne Chicken

SERVES 3 TO 4

1 whole chicken (4 pounds),
cut into 8 pieces (see Simple
Swap)

Kosher salt and freshly ground
black pepper

2 tablespoons extra-virgin
olive oil

1 large yellow onion, halved
through the stem and sliced
¼-inch thick

12 ounces seedless green
grapes, in small clusters on the
stem (about 2½ cups)

4 garlic cloves, minced

2 teaspoons fresh thyme
leaves, plus more for serving

½ cup Champagne or
Prosecco

1 teaspoon Dijon mustard

2 tablespoons heavy cream

SIMPLE SWAP

You should be able to find
whole chickens cut into
8 parts (2 breasts, 2 thighs,
2 wings, and 2 drumsticks)
at most supermarkets, but
if you can't, ask the butcher
to break one down for you.
If you prefer, you can also
make this recipe with
3½ pounds of bone-in,
skin-on chicken thighs.

Make this when you have something to celebrate! Champagne is the perfect wine to pair with this elegant braised chicken, not only beause it's festive but because the bubbles cut right through the creamy, mustardy pan-sauce. And since we're popping bottles, you might as well pour some into the pan to flavor the chicken and plump green grapes that cook alongside it. Of course, you don't have to use Champagne—a good-quality Prosecco works, too. Just pick one you'd enjoy drinking with dinner, and be sure to serve the chicken with lots of crusty bread to mop up the sauce.

1. Preheat the oven to 375°F.

2. Pat the chicken pieces dry with a paper towel and season them all over with 1 teaspoon salt and ½ teaspoon black pepper.

3. In a 12-inch ovenproof skillet, heat the oil over medium heat. Add half the chicken pieces, skin-side down, and cook undisturbed until the skin is golden brown and the chicken releases fairly easily from the pan, 6 to 8 minutes. (Use a splatter screen if you have one.) Flip and cook until browned on the other side, about 3 minutes. Transfer to a plate and repeat with the remaining pieces of chicken.

4. Drain and discard all but a thin layer of fat, about ¼ cup, from the skillet. Add the onion to the pan along with ½ teaspoon salt and a few grinds of black pepper. Cook, tossing often, until the onion is lightly browned, 8 to 10 minutes. Add the grapes, garlic, and thyme and cook for 30 seconds, being careful not to let the garlic burn.

5. Off the heat, add the Champagne and scrape any browned bits from the pan. Return the chicken pieces, skin-side up, along with any accumulated juices to the pan, nestling the larger pieces into the clusters of grapes. Transfer the skillet to the oven and bake until an instant-read thermometer inserted into the thickest part of the breast meat registers 165°F, 20 to 25 minutes.

6. Carefully remove the skillet from the oven and transfer the chicken to a plate to rest while you make the sauce. Add the mustard to the pan juices in the skillet and bring to a simmer over medium heat. Cook for 3 minutes, stirring often, until the liquid has slightly reduced. Stir in the heavy cream and cook for 1 more minute.

7. Spoon the sauce onto the bottom of a large serving platter with raised edges. Thinly slice the chicken breast crosswise and arrange on the platter with the rest of the chicken pieces. Scatter the grapes around the chicken. Sprinkle with salt and black pepper, garnish with a few fresh thyme leaves, and serve.

Date-Night Rib Eye
with Wild Mushrooms

SERVES 2

1½-pound bone-in rib eye steak, about 1½ inches thick

1 tablespoon canola oil

2 teaspoons kosher salt, plus more to taste

¾ teaspoon freshly ground black pepper, plus more to taste

2 tablespoons unsalted butter

2 garlic cloves, smashed flat with the side of a knife

2 fresh rosemary sprigs

12 ounces mixed fresh mushrooms (such as cremini, oyster, and chanterelles), trimmed and chopped or torn into 1-inch pieces

1 tablespoon white or red wine

Minced fresh chives, for serving (optional)

Flaky sea salt, for serving (optional)

Cooking a steak in a skillet always reminds me of my time at The Lost Kitchen in Freedom, Maine. I worked in the restaurant's kitchen for five months as a prep cook, learning everything I could from chef/owner Erin French and her incredible team. Getting to experience the love, creative vision, and hard work that make The Lost Kitchen so special was a formative experience for me.

The restaurant has a set menu each night, and Erin cooks the main course for all fifty diners in quick succession, working six skillets of steak, tuna, or halibut at once, flipping and basting each one with the measured grace of a ballerina. It is truly a sight to behold, and with that image in my mind, I know I can handle one skillet in my own kitchen!

The best part of searing a steak in a skillet is basting it with butter, garlic, and herbs, and it always feels like a crime to leave those delicious juices behind in the pan. In this recipe, I add a handful of wild mushrooms to the skillet while the steak rests, letting them sear in the bubbling butter until perfectly tender and full of meaty flavor.

I call this "date-night" rib eye because it serves two perfectly, and because there's something romantic to me about cooking a big, juicy steak at home. But of course it's delicious any time you make it, shared with anyone who loves a good steak.

1. Allow the steak to sit on the counter for 30 minutes to come to room temperature.

2. Heat a 10-inch stainless steel or cast-iron skillet over medium-high heat for 3 minutes, or until a drop of water flicked into the pan evaporates almost immediately. Rub the canola oil all over the steak and sprinkle with the salt and pepper, making sure to coat both sides.

3. Place the steak in the skillet and press down with a spatula so that it makes good contact with the pan. Cook for 2 minutes, then flip, and cook for 2 minutes on the other side. Repeat two more times, so you've cooked the steak for 4 minutes on each side. Stand the steak up on its fatty side and cook for 30 seconds to let some of the fat render.

4. Lay the steak back down, reduce the heat to medium-low, and add the butter, garlic, and rosemary. Cook for 30 seconds on each side, tilting the pan and spooning the melted butter and fat over the steak. Using tongs, transfer the steak to a cutting board and set aside to rest for 10 minutes.

RECIPE CONTINUES

5. While the steak rests, tilt the pan and carefully spoon out all but a thin layer of fat—about 2 tablespoons—from the skillet, leaving the rosemary and garlic in the pan. Increase the heat to medium-high and add half the mushrooms to the pan in an even layer. Cook for 2 minutes without moving, then toss and continue cooking until the mushrooms are tender, about 2 more minutes. Spoon into a small serving bowl and repeat with the remaining mushrooms. Off the heat, return the first batch of mushrooms to the pan, along with the wine, and toss. Sprinkle with the chives and a pinch of flaky sea salt.

6. Cut the steak into ½-inch-thick slices and serve with the mushrooms on the side.

Grilled Chicken
with Yogurt & Shawarma Spices

SERVES 6

For the chicken

1 teaspoon sweet paprika

1 teaspoon ground cumin

½ teaspoon ground coriander

½ teaspoon ground ginger

½ teaspoon ground turmeric

¼ teaspoon ground allspice

¼ teaspoon ground cinnamon

Kosher salt and freshly ground black pepper

3 tablespoons extra-virgin olive oil, plus more for the grill

1½ cups plain whole-milk yogurt

¼ cup minced yellow onion

2 garlic cloves, grated on a Microplane or minced

3 pounds boneless, skinless chicken breasts and/or thighs

Half a lemon, for serving

Fresh parsley or mint leaves, for serving

If you've ever grilled chicken, you've probably found yourself standing at the grill, worried about taking the chicken off too soon or leaving it on too long. I've been there!

Thankfully, I've figured out two tricks that make grilling chicken foolproof. First, I always buy chicken breasts and thighs on the smaller side. They cook quickly and are tastier, too, because they come from smaller, free-range birds. Second, I like to pound chicken breasts until they are an even thickness throughout—not as thin as I would for schnitzel, but just enough so that one end of the breast isn't significantly thicker than the other. (You can skip that step if you're using thighs here.)

In this recipe, I have a third trick to keep the chicken from getting dry and overcooked. The yogurt in the marinade tenderizes the chicken as it sits and adds a layer of protection between the chicken and the hot grill. That way, the outside of the chicken gets a nice char, while the inside remains moist and tender. The flavors in the marinade are inspired by spices often used in shawarma, the Middle Eastern dish of spit-roasted, thinly sliced meat. I love how the smoky spices complement the char-grilled flavor of the chicken, and how beautifully they pair with this simple tahini-yogurt sauce.

1. Make the marinade: In a large bowl, combine the paprika, cumin, coriander, ginger, turmeric, allspice, cinnamon, 2 teaspoons salt, and ½ teaspoon pepper. Add the olive oil and whisk until smooth. Add the yogurt, onion, and garlic and mix well. Set the marinade aside.

2. Pat the chicken pieces dry with a paper towel. If using breasts, cut the breasts in half crosswise, so you have one thicker, rounded piece and one thinner, triangular piece. Working in batches, place the chicken pieces on a large cutting board and cover them with a sheet of parchment paper. Using a meat mallet or rolling pin, pound the chicken through the paper until each piece is about the same thickness as the others, between ½ and ¾ inch thick. (Be careful not to pound so hard you tear the chicken.)

3. Add the chicken pieces to the marinade and toss well. Cover and refrigerate for at least 3 hours or up to 24.

RECIPE CONTINUES

For the tahini-yogurt sauce

1 cup plain whole-milk yogurt

2 tablespoons tahini

1 tablespoon freshly squeezed lemon juice

Half a medium garlic clove, grated or finely minced

¼ teaspoon kosher salt

4. **Meanwhile, make the tahini-yogurt sauce:** In a small bowl, combine the yogurt, tahini, lemon juice, garlic, and salt. Mix well. Refrigerate for at least 30 minutes (and up to 3 days) until ready to use.

5. Before grilling, let the chicken come to room temperature for 30 minutes. If using a charcoal or gas grill, clean the grates and brush them with oil. Set the grill to medium-high or heat a grill pan slicked with olive oil on the stovetop over medium-high.

6. Lift the chicken from the marinade (no need to brush off excess marinade) and grill until cooked through, 6 to 8 minutes on each side, covering the grill halfway through, if necessary, to retain the heat.

7. Transfer the chicken to a plate, sprinkle generously with salt and squeeze the lemon half over the pieces. Allow the chicken to rest for at least 10 minutes before serving. Garnish with chopped fresh parsley or mint and serve the tahini-yogurt sauce on the side.

LEFTOVERS FOR LUNCH

Leftover grilled chicken would be great on a green salad, or packed into a wrap with cucumbers, tomatoes, lettuce, and extra yogurt sauce.

Spicy Barbecue Pulled Chicken Sandwiches

SERVES 6

For the chicken

2 pounds bone-in, skin-on chicken thighs (4 to 6 thighs)

2 pounds bone-in, skin-on chicken breasts (2 to 4 breasts)

1 teaspoon sweet paprika

½ teaspoon ground cumin

½ teaspoon cayenne pepper

Kosher salt and freshly ground black pepper

¼ cup extra-virgin olive oil

For the barbecue sauce

2 tablespoons extra-virgin olive or canola oil

½ cup minced shallots

1 (12-ounce) bottle stout beer, such as Guinness

¼ cup cider vinegar

¼ cup Worcestershire sauce

⅓ cup tomato paste

¼ cup light or dark brown sugar

3 tablespoons honey

1 tablespoon Dijon mustard

2 garlic cloves, grated on a Microplane

Kosher salt and freshly ground black pepper

½ teaspoons sweet paprika

Pinch of ground cumin

It's tough to beat barbecued pulled pork, braised all day in the oven, but when time is of the essence, I prefer to make pulled chicken. Complete with homemade barbecue sauce, it's cooked to perfection in just under an hour. This is a recipe I originally created for the *New York Times*, and I make it so often that I knew I had to include the recipe in this book. Summer cookout, football game, snow day—whatever the occasion, this one's a major crowd-pleaser. I like to set out a spread of buns, chicken, and coleslaw and let everyone assemble their own sandwiches.

Finally, I just want to note that this chicken does have a kick, so if you're cooking for kids, or the otherwise spice-averse, you may want to cut the cayenne pepper in half.

1. Preheat the oven to 375°F.

2. Pat the chicken thighs and breasts dry and place them on a sheet pan, skin-side up. In a small bowl, combine the paprika, cumin, cayenne, 2 teaspoons salt, and 1 teaspoon black pepper. Whisk in the olive oil, then pour over the chicken and toss to coat.

3. Roast for 35 to 45 minutes, depending on the size of the pieces, until an instant-read thermometer registers 165°F in both the thighs and breasts. Set aside until cool enough to handle, reserving the pan drippings.

4. **Meanwhile, make the barbecue sauce:** In a medium saucepan, heat the olive oil over medium heat. Add the shallots and cook, stirring occasionally, until tender, 3 to 5 minutes. Add the beer, vinegar, Worcestershire sauce, tomato paste, brown sugar, honey, mustard, garlic, 1 teaspoon salt, ½ teaspoon black pepper, the paprika, and cumin and whisk until smooth. Bring to a boil, then reduce the heat to medium-low and cook, stirring occasionally, until reduced and thickened, 25 to 30 minutes.

5. When the chicken is cool enough to handle, remove the meat from the thighs and breasts, discarding the bones and skin. Tear the meat into bite-size pieces and place in a large bowl. Add a few tablespoons of the reserved drippings and toss to coat.

6. Add the chicken to the sauce and toss well. If necessary, rewarm over medium-low heat. (If making in advance, transfer the chicken and sauce to an airtight container and refrigerate for up to 3 days. Reheat in a saucepan set over medium heat before serving, or partially covered in a 350°F oven for 20 minutes.)

7. Serve with hamburger buns, coleslaw, and pickles and let everyone assemble their own sandwiches.

For serving

6 hamburger buns

Perfect Picnic Coleslaw
(page 170)

Pickle slices

GET AHEAD
This is even more delicious reheated the next day, once the chicken has had plenty of time in the sauce, so it's an ideal recipe to make in advance.

COOKING FOR A CROWD
I love to make this for big summer parties, in part because I can make the whole thing ahead of time (see above). When doubling the recipe, I cook the chicken on two sheet pans to avoid overcrowding, and I simmer the barbecue sauce for a few extra minutes if necessary.

Spicy Barbecue Pulled Chicken Sandwiches, page 96

Orecchiette with White Bolognese

SERVES 4 TO 6

Kosher salt and freshly ground black pepper

4 ounces cubed pancetta

8 ounces cremini mushrooms, ½-inch diced

2 tablespoons unsalted butter

1 medium yellow onion, chopped

1½ cups (½-inch) diced carrots (2 to 3 medium carrots)

1 cup (½-inch) diced celery (about 2 celery ribs)

1 teaspoon fennel seeds

1 teaspoon dried oregano

¼ teaspoon crushed red pepper flakes, plus more for serving

2 tablespoons minced garlic (4 large cloves)

1 pound ground pork

1 cup dry white wine, such as Pinot Grigio

1 cup low-sodium chicken broth or water

⅓ cup heavy cream

1 pound orecchiette pasta

Grated Parmesan cheese, for serving

¼ cup chopped fresh parsley

This idea for a riff on traditional Bolognese comes from my friend Simon. Simon is one of the most naturally gifted people I know—he can sing, draw, paint, and take a casual iPhone photo that looks like a work of art. His creativity extends to cooking, too. Simon and I often bounce ideas off each other, and one day, as we were chatting on the phone while making dinner in our respective kitchens, he told me about a white Bolognese he'd made that week. He listed the ingredients and said, "I basically just cooked it all together into a sauce." Okay, maybe recipe writing isn't one of his gifts. But I loved the idea and played around with it, organizing it into recipe form so you, too, can make it!

Unlike a classic Bolognese, white Bolognese doesn't have any tomatoes. Instead, it leans on pancetta, sautéed vegetables, white wine, and a splash of cream to make a complex, flavorful sauce. It's a luxurious spin on a classic and is absolutely delicious served with a Simple Green Salad (page 263) and a glass of white wine.

1. Bring a large pot of salted water to a boil.

2. Meanwhile, heat a 10-inch Dutch oven over medium heat. Once hot, cook the pancetta until browned, 3 to 5 minutes.

3. Add the mushrooms and cook, tossing occasionally, until they release their water and the liquid in the pan evaporates, about 3 minutes. Add the butter, onion, carrots, celery, fennel seeds, oregano, and pepper flakes and cook, stirring occasionally, until the vegetables are tender, 6 to 8 minutes. Add the garlic and cook for 1 more minute, until fragrant.

4. Add the pork, 2 teaspoons salt, and ½ teaspoon black pepper and cook, breaking up the meat into chunks with a wooden spoon, until browned, about 4 minutes.

5. Add the wine and bring to a simmer over medium heat, scraping any browned bits from the bottom of the pan. Add the broth and cream and bring to a boil. Reduce the heat and simmer, uncovered, until slightly reduced and thickened, about 15 minutes. Set aside off the heat.

6. Add the pasta to the boiling water and cook until al dente according to the package directions.

7. Return the sauce to low heat. Reserving 1 cup of pasta water, drain the pasta and add it to the sauce. Toss well, adding a splash of pasta water if needed to loosen up the sauce.

8. Serve hot with Parmesan and a sprinkle of parsley.

Grilled Skirt Steak with Romesco Salsa

SERVES 6

For the steak

2 pounds skirt steak

⅓ cup extra-virgin olive oil

2 tablespoons red wine vinegar

3 garlic cloves, minced

2 teaspoons light brown sugar

¼ teaspoon cayenne pepper

Kosher salt and freshly ground black pepper

For the romesco salsa

1 tablespoon extra-virgin olive oil

½ cup raw almonds, coarsely chopped

1 cup cherry tomatoes, chopped

1 cup jarred roasted red peppers, drained and chopped

1 tablespoon red wine vinegar

¼ cup chopped fresh parsley

2 garlic cloves, minced or grated

¼ teaspoon smoked paprika

¼ teaspoon kosher salt

Romesco is a pureed sauce made with tomatoes, roasted red peppers, olive oil, garlic, almonds, and parsley that originated in the Catalan region of Spain. It's almost like a smoky Spanish pesto, and it's one of my favorite sauces to eat with any kind of simply cooked meat or fish.

One night when I was making a batch of romesco, I was struck by how pretty the ingredients looked together before they were blended and decided to try making a rustic salsa with them. I never looked back. As the saying goes, we eat with our eyes, and I think there's something extra delicious about seeing the little pieces of peppers, tomatoes, almonds, and parsley in each bite.

Piled on top of grilled skirt steak, this salsa turns this everyday cut of meat into a total showstopper. It's also delicious on grilled or seared salmon, or served alongside a roast chicken.

1. If necessary, cut the steak crosswise into pieces that are 6 to 8 inches long. In a large, bowl, whisk together the olive oil, vinegar, garlic, brown sugar, cayenne, 1 teaspoon salt, and ¼ teaspoon black pepper. Add the steak and toss well to coat. Cover the bowl with plastic wrap and refrigerate for at least 3 hours or up to 24.

2. When you're ready to cook the steak, remove it from the fridge and allow it to come to room temperature on the counter for 30 minutes.

3. **Meanwhile, make the salsa:** Heat a small skillet over medium-low heat. Add the olive oil and then the almonds and cook, tossing often, until the almonds are fragrant and just beginning to brown, about 3 minutes. (Be careful not to let them burn!) Remove from the heat and using a slotted spoon, transfer to a small bowl to cool.

4. In a medium bowl, combine the tomatoes, roasted peppers, vinegar, parsley, garlic, paprika, and salt. Toss and set aside.

5. Set the grill to medium-high heat (or heat a grill pan on the stovetop over medium-high). Cook the steak for 3 to 5 minutes on each side, depending on the thickness of each piece, for medium-rare and watching out for flare-ups. Transfer to a plate, sprinkle lightly with salt, and allow to rest for 10 minutes.

6. While the steak rests, drain all but a few tablespoons of liquid from the salsa with a small spoon. (The amount of liquid will depend on how long the salsa has been sitting and how juicy the tomatoes are.) Add the almonds and toss.

RECIPE CONTINUES ON PAGE 105

7. To serve, slice the steak crosswise into 3-inch pieces, then slice against the grain to cut the steak into wide strips. Arrange the sliced steak on a large flat platter, then spoon about half the salsa on top. Serve with the rest of the salsa on the side.

TIP

I always recommend skirt steak to grilling beginners. It's relatively inexpensive, it cooks quickly, and it absorbs marinades beautifully. The trick is to remember to slice the cooked steak against the grain into long strips. The "grain" refers to the natural muscle fibers—or lines that appear in pieces of beef. You may be tempted to slice with the grain, but cutting perpendicular to it is crucial to tenderize this lean cut of meat.

Roast Chicken with Cipollini Onions, White Beans & Lemon

SERVES 4

1 (4-pound) chicken, giblets removed

12 ounces cipollini or pearl onions

4 garlic cloves, unpeeled

1 large lemon, quartered

3 (4-inch) fresh rosemary sprigs

Extra-virgin olive oil

Kosher salt and freshly ground black pepper

1 (15-ounce) can cannellini beans, rinsed and drained

One of the first things Ina showed me how to make was, of course, a good roast chicken. To this day, it's one of the most comforting, cozy dinners I know. Typically, I'll use whatever herbs and veggies I have on hand, but when I'm planning ahead, I roast the chicken in a skillet on top of garlic cloves, cipollini onions, and lemons. Then, while the chicken rests, I add a can of rinsed white beans right to the skillet. Gently heated with the pan juices, lemon juice, and roasted garlic, the beans become a built-in side dish that makes the most of every ingredient in the pan.

Carving a chicken takes some practice, but like anything else, the more you do it, the easier it will become. Let the chicken rest for longer than you think you should—a good 15 to 20 minutes. Not only will the meat be juicier, but it's much easier to carve a chicken that isn't piping hot.

1. Preheat the oven to 400°F, letting the chicken sit at room temperature while the oven heats.

2. Trim both ends of the onions and place them in a bowl of hot tap water for a minute or two. (This will make it easier to remove the skins.) Peel the onions, and cut any larger than 1 inch in half through the stem. Place them in a 12-inch ovenproof stainless steel skillet or other baking dish just large enough to hold the chicken. (If there is too much room around the chicken, the vegetables may burn.)

3. Add the garlic, 2 of the lemon quarters, and 1 of the rosemary sprigs to the pan. Drizzle with 1 tablespoon olive oil and toss well. Push the vegetables to the edges of the pan, creating space for the chicken in the center.

4. Pat the chicken dry with paper towels and place it breast-side up in the pan. Season the chicken all over, including the cavity, with 2 teaspoons salt and ½ teaspoon pepper. Stuff the remaining 2 lemon quarters and 2 rosemary sprigs into the cavity and tie the legs together with kitchen string. (If you don't have string, you can skip this step!) Drizzle another tablespoon of olive oil over the chicken and use your hands or a pastry brush to make sure the skin is coated in oil.

5. Transfer the skillet to the oven and roast for 30 minutes.

6. Gently toss the onions. Return the pan to the oven and roast until the juices run clear when a knife is inserted between the leg and the thigh, about 45 more minutes.

7. Using a large spatula, carefully transfer the chicken to a board and set it aside to rest for at least 15 minutes. Leave the oven on.

8. Meanwhile, press the garlic cloves with a fork to remove the skins. Discard the skins and mash the roasted garlic with a fork, mixing it into the pan juices. Press the lemons to release their juices, then add the white beans to the skillet and toss. Return to the oven for 5 to 10 minutes to heat the beans through. Taste and season with more salt and pepper if desired.

9. Carve the chicken and arrange the pieces on a platter. Spoon the beans and pan juices around it, and serve.

LEFTOVERS FOR LUNCH

If you're lucky enough to have leftover chicken (even scraps!) you are on your way to a delicious lunch. Chop any remaining chicken into bite-size pieces and remove whatever meat you can from the chicken bones. Add mayonnaise, a squeeze of lemon or vinegar, a handful of chopped herbs, and salt and pepper for a quick and classic chicken salad. Oh, and save that carcass for a batch of homemade chicken broth (see page 259)!

Shortcut Chicken Schnitzel

SERVES 4

4 thinly sliced chicken breast cutlets (4 to 6 ounces each)

Kosher salt and freshly ground black pepper

½ cup all-purpose flour

2 large eggs, lightly beaten

1 tablespoon Dijon mustard

2 teaspoons Worcestershire sauce

2 cups panko bread crumbs

½ cup canola or other neutral oil, divided, plus more as needed

Flaky sea salt, for serving

Lemon wedges, for serving

I love chicken schnitzel, but when I make it at home, I somehow manage to use every cutting board, plate, and bowl in the kitchen, along with an entire roll of paper towels. While there isn't really any way around the breading and frying, I do have a little shortcut for taking the most labor-intensive step—the pounding—out of the equation. By starting with thinly sliced chicken breasts, you can skip the meat mallet and go right to the good stuff, getting the chicken in the pan, and on the plate, with a little bit less mess in your wake. Don't be skimpy with the oil here; keeping a generous amount of oil in the pan at all times will ensure your schnitzel comes out perfectly golden and crispy.

1. Pat the chicken breasts dry with a paper towel and season generously with salt and pepper.

2. Set up three large shallow bowls on the counter, and place the flour in one bowl. In the second bowl, beat the eggs, mustard, and Worcestershire sauce with a fork until smooth. Place the panko in the third bowl and with your hands, crush a few handfuls of crumbs to give them a slightly finer texture.

3. Working with one cutlet at a time, dip the chicken into the flour, shaking off any excess, then into the eggs, and finally, the panko. Place the prepared breasts on a clean plate until ready to use.

4. Line a sheet pan with paper towels and have it at the ready. In a 12-inch skillet, heat ¼ cup of the oil over medium-high heat. When the oil is hot (it should sizzle if you flick a bit of water into the pan), place 2 chicken cutlets in the pan. Cook, pressing the chicken lightly with a spatula, until golden brown on both sides and cooked through, 2 to 3 minutes per side. (You may need to reduce the heat to medium if the chicken begins browning too quickly.) Transfer to the paper towels and sprinkle with flaky salt.

5. Wipe out the skillet with a paper towel, add the remaining ¼ cup oil, and repeat the process with the other 2 cutlets, adjusting the heat as necessary.

6. Serve the chicken hot with lemon wedges on the side.

MAKE IT A MEAL

I often serve this recipe with my Green Beans with Crispy Capers & Garlic (page 157), sautéing the beans in the skillet first before wiping it out and using it to cook the chicken.

LEFTOVERS FOR LUNCH

Even when I'm cooking for two, I make a full recipe so we'll have leftovers the next day. I like to cut leftover schnitzel into strips and add them to a salad for a perfect lunch.

Braised Short Ribs
with Port, Shallots & Cranberries

5 pounds bone-in beef short ribs (see Tip), about 1½ inches thick by 3 inches

Kosher salt and freshly ground black pepper

2 tablespoons neutral oil, such as grapeseed or canola oil

1 pound shallots, trimmed and cut lengthwise into ¾-inch wedges (about 8 medium shallots)

2 tablespoons minced garlic (about 5 large cloves)

2 tablespoons tomato paste

1½ cups tawny port

2 to 4 cups low-sodium beef broth, as needed

⅓ cup freshly squeezed orange juice (1 to 2 oranges)

¼ cup honey

3 tablespoons Worcestershire sauce

½ teaspoon ground allspice

1½ cups frozen cranberries

2 fresh rosemary sprigs

This recipe is my go-to winter showstopper—the perfect festive centerpiece for a holiday dinner or other cold-weather feast. Like any good braised short ribs, these are rich, meaty, and incredibly tender. But what makes them extra-special are the port and the fresh cranberries, which lend the sauce a subtle sweetness.

I like to serve these short ribs over Creamy Polenta (page 162) with a bright green salad on the side. If you plan to cook the ribs just before serving them, make sure to give yourself plenty of time; the sauce needs half an hour to reduce after the ribs are done braising. (See Tip for making this recipe in advance!)

1. Preheat the oven to 300°F.

2. Trim any exterior fat from the short ribs and season all over with 2 teaspoons salt and 1 teaspoon pepper.

3. In a 10-inch Dutch oven, heat the oil over medium-high heat. Working in batches to avoid crowding, cook the short ribs until browned on all sides, 8 to 10 minutes. Transfer to a plate.

4. Drain all but about 2 tablespoons of fat from the pot. Reduce the heat to medium, add the shallots, and cook, tossing occasionally, until browned all over, 4 to 6 minutes. Add the garlic and cook for 30 seconds, until fragrant. (Be careful not to let the garlic burn.) Add the tomato paste and cook for 2 minutes, stirring occasionally, until it darkens in color.

5. Add the port, bring to a simmer, and cook for 1 minute, scraping any browned bits from the pan. Add 2 cups of the broth, the orange juice, honey, Worcestershire sauce, allspice, 1 teaspoon salt, and ½ teaspoon pepper and stir. Return the short ribs to the pot, nestling them into the liquid. If necessary, add more broth so that the short ribs are completely submerged.

6. Bring to a simmer, then cover the pot, transfer to the oven, and bake for 1½ hours.

7. Stir in the cranberries and rosemary, partially cover, return to the oven, and bake until the meat is fork-tender, about 1 more hour. The meat should be falling off the bone.

RECIPE CONTINUES

8. Transfer the short ribs to a plate and set aside. Skim off as much fat as you can from the surface of the sauce with a large spoon. Take your time and don't worry if a bit of the sauce comes with the fat. Discard the fat and bring the sauce to a boil over medium-high heat. Reduce the heat slightly and simmer vigorously, stirring occasionally, until thickened and reduced by about three-quarters, 25 to 30 minutes.

9. Return the short ribs to the pot and heat through over low heat. Serve hot. (Or cool completely and refrigerate for up to 48 hours; see Get Ahead.)

TIP

Short ribs often have a thick layer of fat on top. Choose short ribs with as little fat as possible, and if the only short ribs available do have a thick fat cap, buy an extra pound to make sure you have enough meat after you trim it.

SIMPLE SWAP

If you can't find port, you can substitute 1½ cups full-bodied red wine, such as Côtes du Rhône or Cabernet Sauvignon, and ½ to 1 teaspoon sugar, depending on the sweetness of the wine.

GET AHEAD

Braised short ribs are a great dish to make a day in advance. If you're going this route, let the short ribs cool completely after you've reduced the braising liquid. Then put the pan, covered, into the fridge. Reheat, covered, over low heat, adding a splash of water to loosen the sauce if necessary.

Fish & Shellfish

Saucy Shrimp alla Vodka 118

Roasted Fish with Green Herbs, Lemon & Olives 121

Salmon with Honey & Chili Crunch 122

Littleneck Clams with Cherry Tomatoes
& Pearl Couscous 125

Slow-Roasted Salmon with Lemony Leeks
& Asparagus 126

Saucy Shrimp alla Vodka

SERVES 4

2 tablespoons unsalted butter or extra-virgin olive oil

2 medium shallots, chopped (½ cup)

1 tablespoon minced garlic (2 large cloves)

½ teaspoon dried oregano

¼ teaspoon crushed red pepper flakes, plus more to taste

2 tablespoons tomato paste

⅓ cup plus 1 tablespoon vodka, divided

1 (15-ounce) can crushed tomatoes

Kosher salt and freshly ground black pepper

1 pound shrimp (16/20 count), peeled and deveined (tails on or off)

¼ cup heavy cream

⅓ cup grated Parmesan cheese

Chopped fresh parsley, for serving

Crusty bread, for serving

When I'm in the mood for something cozy, quick, and comforting but not necessarily a big bowl of pasta, this recipe fits the bill perfectly. Vodka sauce is incredibly easy to make at home and uses mostly pantry staples (vodka's a pantry staple, right?) Traditionally, Italians don't eat seafood and cheese together, but as far as I know pasta alla vodka is a distinctly Italian American creation, so I think we can let this one slide. The delicate, briny flavor of the shrimp makes them an absolutely delicious (if rule-breaking) partner to the creamy vodka sauce.

1. In a 12-inch skillet, melt the butter over medium-low heat. Add the shallots and cook, stirring occasionally, until translucent, 3 to 5 minutes. Add the garlic, oregano, and pepper flakes and cook until the garlic is fragrant, about 1 minute.

2. Add the tomato paste and cook, stirring occasionally, until the paste has darkened in color and turned the butter bright orange, 2 to 3 minutes.

3. Increase the heat to medium and add ⅓ cup of the vodka. Cook until the liquid has almost completely evaporated. Add the tomatoes, 1 teaspoon salt, and a few grinds of black pepper. Bring to a boil, then reduce the heat and simmer, stirring occasionally, for 10 to 12 minutes, until the sauce is thickened.

4. While the sauce is cooking, pat the shrimp dry with a paper towel and sprinkle them with salt and pepper.

5. Add the shrimp to the skillet and cook until they are just beginning to become opaque, about 3 minutes. Stir in the heavy cream and simmer until the shrimp are just cooked through, about 1 more minute.

6. Off the heat, stir in the remaining 1 tablespoon vodka and the Parmesan. Taste for seasonings, and serve hot sprinkled with the parsley, with crusty bread on the side.

MAKE IT A MEAL
Serve the shrimp in shallow pasta bowls or straight from the skillet, with lots of bread for dipping. If you want to go full red-sauce joint, add a bottle of Chianti and some Roasted Broccolini with Pickled Pepperoncini (page 173) on the side.

Roasted Fish
with Green Herbs, Lemon & Olives

SERVES 4

4 skinless halibut (6 ounces each), at least 1-inch thick

⅓ cup extra-virgin olive oil, plus more for drizzling

3 tablespoons minced fresh tarragon leaves

3 tablespoons minced fresh chives

1 tablespoon chopped fresh thyme leaves

Kosher salt and freshly ground black pepper

1 lemon

⅔ cup pitted Castelvetrano or other green olives

This recipe comes from my mother-in-law, Mary. She's taught me a lot of great cooking tricks and is an absolute force in the kitchen. You know Mary is cooking when you walk into the house and the music is pumping at full volume. I've changed some of the seasonings and herbs, but the timing and technique here are all hers. This is an easy, totally hands-off method of cooking fish, which makes it an ideal recipe for new or nervous cooks—for all cooks, really!

1. Preheat the oven to 400°F.

2. Pat the fish dry with a paper towel and place the fillets on a plate on the counter while you prepare the herb oil.

3. In a small bowl, whisk together the olive oil, tarragon, chives, thyme, 1½ teaspoons salt, and a few grinds of black pepper. Grate the lemon zest into the bowl and whisk well. Cut the lemon into quarters. Remove any visible seeds and set aside.

4. Drizzle a thin layer, about 2 tablespoons olive oil, onto the bottom of a baking dish large enough to fit the fillets without crowding. Add the olives and lemon quarters and toss to coat with olive oil. Add the fish, spacing them evenly in the pan. Brush the herb oil all over the top and sides of the fillets.

5. Roast until the fish is cooked through and flakes easily with a fork, 18 to 22 minutes, depending on the thickness of the fillets. Press the lemon quarters gently with the back of a spoon to release their juice, then carefully tilt the pan and spoon the pan juices over the fish.

6. Carefully transfer the fish to a serving dish, along with the olives. Sprinkle lightly with salt and serve hot.

SIMPLE SWAP

Halibut is my favorite fish to use in this recipe, but when it's too expensive or unavailable, fluke or cod are great substitutes. Just try to get fillets around the same size so they cook evenly.

COOKING FOR A CROWD

This recipe scales up beautifully. You can cook up to 12 fillets on a standard sheet pan (multiplying the ingredients accordingly), and the cooking time will remain the same.

Salmon
with Honey & Chili Crunch

SERVES 2

2 skinless salmon fillets
(6 ounces each)

Kosher salt

1 tablespoon Momofuku Chili
Crunch or chili crisp

1 teaspoon rice vinegar

1 tablespoon honey

When time is of the essence—which, really, is most nights—it's helpful to have a few go-to dishes that come together in just a few minutes and don't require a scavenger hunt at the grocery store. This salmon recipe is one I make often, knowing I have all the ingredients except the salmon waiting for me at home.

The secret ingredient is a jar of Momofuku's Chili Crunch—a crunchy, spicy, saucy condiment inspired by Chinese chili oil and Mexican salsa macha. Mixed with honey and a splash of vinegar, it makes a spicy, flavor-packed glaze that really stands up to salmon's rich flavor. My friend Marguerite has worked at Momofuku for over ten years and always beings us a fresh jar of Chili Crunch when she comes to visit.

I like to serve this salmon with steamed white rice, and simply steamed broccoli or Crunchy Cucumber Salad with Peanuts & Chili Flakes (page 161), mixing any extra glaze with the veggies. And while I've written this recipe for 2 servings, it multiplies well and even works cut in half to serve one.

1. Preheat the oven to 375°F and line a sheet pan with parchment paper.

2. Pat the salmon dry with a paper towel, sprinkle all over with salt, and place on the prepared pan.

3. In a small bowl, combine the Chili Crunch and vinegar and whisk with a fork until well combined. Add the honey and whisk again. Using a pastry brush or a small spoon, spread the glaze all over the top and sides of the salmon.

4. Roast until the salmon is just cooked through and flakes easily at the edges, 12 to 14 minutes, depending on the thickness of the fillets. Spoon any glaze that has collected on the pan back over the fish. Serve hot or warm.

SIMPLE SWAP

Momofuku Chili Crunch is sold in most large grocery stores and online at momofuku.com, but in a pinch, jarred chili crisp works, too.

Littleneck Clams
with Cherry Tomatoes & Pearl Couscous

SERVES 3 TO 4

3 pounds littleneck clams

Kosher salt and freshly
ground black pepper

3 tablespoons extra-virgin
olive oil

2 large shallots, chopped
(about ¾ cup)

4 garlic cloves, minced

1 small red chile, such as
Fresno or red jalapeño,
seeded and minced (about
1 tablespoon)

1 pint sungold or other orange
cherry tomatoes

1 cup red cherry tomatoes

½ cup dry white wine, such as
Sauvignon Blanc

½ cup pearl couscous or
fregola

2 tablespoons chopped fresh
parsley

Crusty bread, for serving

COOKING FOR A CROWD

The only thing standing
between you and a double
batch of these clams is a
huge pot! Use a very large
(8-quart or larger) Dutch
oven or pasta pot that gives
you enough room to toss the
clams easily.

There are few meals more summery than a seafood feast at home. When
you're lucky enough to have access to good-quality fresh seafood, this is
the recipe to make. Clams may seem intimidating if you haven't worked
with them before, but I promise they are actually really easy to cook! This
whole dish is made in one pan, and doesn't require any special equipment or
techniques, just a bit of simmering and stirring.

As the clams open up, they release their salty, briny "liquor," which forms
the base of the broth here, along with sweet cherry tomatoes, garlic, white
wine, and shallots. Everything cooks together, forming the most delicious,
fragrant sauce that's just begging to be mopped up with a piece of bread.

The couscous gives this recipe enough heft to be a main course, but
it can easily be stretched to serve 6 as a first course if you're planning a full
seafood extravaganza.

1. Place the clams in a large bowl, along with 1 tablespoon salt, and fill the bowl
with cold water. Set aside for 30 minutes to let the clams release any grit. Lift the
clams from the water, and rinse well under running water, scrubbing if necessary.

2. In a large Dutch oven, or a deep 12-inch skillet with a lid, heat the olive oil
over medium heat. Add the shallots and cook, stirring occasionally, until tender
but not browned, 3 to 5 minutes. Add the garlic and chile and cook until fragrant,
30 seconds to 1 minute.

3. Add both the sungold and red cherry tomatoes, ½ teaspoon salt, and a few
grinds of black pepper and cook over medium heat, stirring occasionally, until the
tomatoes have begun to collapse, 6 to 8 minutes.

4. Add the wine and bring to a boil. Reduce the heat to medium-low and add the
clams, nestling them into the sauce and spreading them into one layer as much as
possible. Cover and cook until the clams open, 8 to 12 minutes, checking every few
minutes and removing clams and placing them in a large bowl as they open. (This
will prevent the clams from overcooking.) Discard any clams that do not open.

5. Bring the liquid in the pan back to a boil and add the couscous. Reduce the heat
and simmer, uncovered, until the couscous is tender and the liquid in the pan has
reduced, 10 to 15 minutes.

6. Off the heat, taste for seasonings and add more salt and pepper to taste.
Carefully pour the tomatoes, couscous, and sauce over the clams. Garnish with the
parsley and serve immediately, with crusty bread on the side.

Slow-Roasted Salmon
with Lemony Leeks & Asparagus

SERVES 6

2 medium leeks, dark green leaves trimmed

1 lemon, very thinly sliced

5 tablespoons extra-virgin olive oil, divided

Kosher salt and freshly ground black pepper

2-pound salmon fillet (see Tip), skin removed

1 pound asparagus, trimmed and cut into ¾-inch pieces

Flaky sea salt, for serving

Fresh dill, for serving

Grated lemon zest, for serving

TIP

If you use a center-cut piece of salmon, it will be cooked evenly the whole way through. If you use a more tapered piece (pictured here) the ends will be slightly more well done than the center. Both work great, but I often ask for a tapered piece if I know some people prefer their salmon on the well-done side (hi, Mom!).

Slow-roasting is a wonderfully forgiving method of cooking salmon. The fish comes out incredibly tender, and because the oven never gets super hot, it's a lot harder to overcook.

In this recipe, I start by roasting leeks and asparagus on a sheet pan and then make some room for the salmon. The pan goes back into the oven until the fish is just cooked through, and then I finish it off with a sprinkle of lemon zest, black pepper, and lots of fresh dill. Salmon perfection, with a built-in side!

This salmon would be delicious as part of a Mother's Day or Easter spread, but it's also simple and fast enough for a weeknight.

1. Preheat the oven to 325°F.

2. Thinly slice the leek crosswise into ¼-inch-thick rounds. Place the leeks in a large bowl of water, swish them around to loosen any grit, then lift them out with a slotted spoon and transfer to a colander to drain. Pat the leeks dry with a clean kitchen towel and spread them out on a sheet pan.

3. Add the lemon slices to the sheet pan. Drizzle the leek and lemon with 2 tablespoons of the olive oil and sprinkle with ½ teaspoon kosher salt and a few grinds of black pepper.

4. Transfer to the oven and roast until the leeks are tender and lightly caramelized, about 30 minutes, tossing twice throughout.

5. Meanwhile, pat the salmon dry and set aside at room temperature.

6. Add the asparagus to the sheet pan along with another 1 tablespoon of the olive oil and ¼ teaspoon salt. Toss well, then push the vegetables to the edges of the pan to create space for the salmon. Place the salmon on the pan, rub all over with the remaining 2 tablespoons olive oil and sprinkle with 1 teaspoon salt and ½ teaspoon pepper.

7. Return to the oven and roast until the salmon registers 120 to 125°F on an instant-read thermometer and flakes easily with a fork, 15 to 25 minutes, depending on the thickness of the fillet. (Because the salmon is cooked so gently in this method, it may still look slightly translucent on top—that's okay!)

8. Transfer the salmon and vegetables to a platter, arranging the vegetables around the fish. Sprinkle the salmon with flaky salt, dill, and lemon zest. Serve warm or at room temperature.

Veggie
Mains

White Bean & Mushroom Cassoulet with
Gruyère Bread Crumbs 132

Cheesy Stuffed Squash with Kale & Brown Rice 136

Spaghetti with Sweet Corn Pesto 138

Red Curry Lentils with Sweet Potato & Spinach 141

Crispy Cauliflower & Chickpea Cakes
with Moroccan Spices 142

White Bean & Mushroom Cassoulet with Gruyère Bread Crumbs

SERVES 6 TO 8

1 ounce dried porcini mushrooms

3 cups very hot tap water

4 tablespoons unsalted butter, divided

1 large Vidalia or other yellow onion, chopped

1 cup (¼-inch) diced carrots (about 2 medium carrots)

1 cup (¼-inch) diced celery (about 2 ribs)

8 ounces cremini mushrooms, trimmed and ¾-inch diced

2 tablespoons minced garlic (4 large cloves)

2 teaspoons fresh thyme leaves

1 tablespoon tomato paste

½ cup dry white wine, such as Sauvignon Blanc

3 (15-ounce) cans cannellini beans, drained and rinsed

Kosher salt and freshly ground black pepper

3 tablespoons dry sherry

2 tablespoons extra-virgin olive oil

2 cups panko bread crumbs

1 cup grated Gruyère or Comté cheese (3 ounces)

¼ cup chopped fresh parsley

In cassoulet—the rustic French stew of braised white beans, sausage, duck confit, and pork—meat takes center stage. The idea of a vegetarian cassoulet might, therefore, sound like an oxymoron, but it has always intrigued me. The base of cassoulet is already white beans—why not swap in some mushrooms for the meat and see how it goes? Turns out, it's delicious!

Dried porcini mushrooms give the broth a ton of flavor, and the vegetables and white beans become incredibly tender as they simmer away with fresh herbs, garlic, and white wine. I also took the liberty of adding a crunchy, cheesy breadcrumb topping to give this cassoulet all the richness of its inspiration. It might be not traditional, but it makes this dish truly special in its own right.

This recipe makes a really nice vegetarian main for a holiday meal, or a comforting dinner any cold night of the year.

1. Preheat the oven to 325°F.

2. Place the dried mushrooms in a medium bowl and add the hot water. Set aside for at least 15 minutes, then lift out the mushrooms, squeezing them over the bowl to extract excess liquid. Finely chop the mushrooms and set aside. Line a fine-mesh sieve with cheesecloth and pour the mushroom broth through it into another medium bowl or liquid measuring cup to remove any grit.

3. Meanwhile, in an 11-inch Dutch oven, melt 2 tablespoons of the butter over medium-low heat. Add the onion and cook, stirring occasionally, until beginning to caramelize, 10 to 15 minutes.

4. Add the remaining 2 tablespoons butter, the carrots, celery, and fresh mushrooms and cook, stirring occasionally, until the mushrooms have begun to release their water, 6 to 8 minutes. Add the garlic and thyme and cook for 1 more minute, until fragrant.

5. Add the tomato paste and cook, stirring occasionally, until the paste darkens in color, 2 to 3 minutes. Add the wine and stir, scraping any browned bits from the bottom of the pot. Add the mushroom broth, the chopped rehydrated mushrooms, the beans, 1 tablespoon salt, and a few grinds of black pepper and bring to a boil over medium-high heat. Reduce the heat to a simmer and cook for 5 minutes, stirring occasionally.

RECIPE CONTINUES ON PAGE 135

6. Transfer the pot to the oven and cook, uncovered, for 45 minutes.

7. Stir to break up the crust that's formed on top, stir in the sherry, then return to the oven for 45 minutes, until the crust has reformed and most of the liquid has evaporated.

8. Meanwhile, in a large bowl, toss together the olive oil and panko. Add the Gruyère, parsley, ½ teaspoon salt, and a few grinds of black pepper and toss well.

9. Turn the oven to broil. Sprinkle the panko mixture evenly over the surface of the cassoulet and broil until the bread crumbs are golden brown and the cheese is melted, 3 to 5 minutes.

10. Cool for 10 minutes, then serve.

GET AHEAD

This cassoulet may be made up to a day in advance, minus the bread crumb topping. Reheat, partially covered, in a 350°F for 25 minutes, then resume the recipe starting at step 8.

Cheesy Stuffed Squash with Kale & Brown Rice

4 honeynut squash (about 12 ounces each) or 3 delicata squash (1 pound each)

3 tablespoons extra-virgin olive oil, divided

Kosher salt and freshly ground black pepper

1 cup chopped yellow onion

4 garlic cloves, minced

3 tablespoons chopped fresh sage

⅛ teaspoon crushed red pepper flakes

⅓ cup dry white wine

3 cups chopped kale leaves

1½ cups cooked brown rice

1½ cups grated Fontina Val d'Aosta cheese, divided (6 ounces)

½ cup grated pecorino cheese, divided

Freshly grated nutmeg, for serving (optional)

TIP

Honeynut squash are a smaller, sweeter cousins of the butternut squash. They're increasingly available at grocery stores and farmers' markets, but if you can't find them, delicata squash are a great substitute.

GET AHEAD

If you want to prep ahead of time, you can assemble the squash in advance and just bake them off before dinner.

I have admitted that my mom was not the world's best cook, but I want to go on the record and say that there *were* a few things she made that I really loved. What she lacked in range, she more than made up for in the things she did well. One was her Bisquick coffee cake, and another was her baked acorn squash with raisins, walnuts, and apples. As a kid, it felt like such a treat to have a squash "boat" all to myself. Maybe it's nostalgia, but I still love any food that is individually portioned, like a personal pot pie or crème brûlée.

These baked squash are inspired by my mom's. Her acorn squash was always a side dish, but these are hearty enough to be a main course on their own. Stuffed with brown rice, kale, sage, and lots of shredded cheese, they make a delicious, satisfying dinner for vegetarians and omnivores alike.

1. Preheat the oven to 400°F and line a sheet pan with parchment paper.

2. Cut the squash in half lengthwise through the stem and scoop out the seeds. Brush the cut sides of the squash with 1 tablespoon of the olive oil and season generously with salt and black pepper. Place the squash, cut-sides down, on the prepared pan and roast until tender when pierced with a fork, 20 to 25 minutes. Set aside until cool enough to handle, leaving the oven on.

3. Meanwhile, in a large (12-inch) skillet, heat the remaining 2 tablespoons olive oil over medium-heat. Add the onion and cook, stirring occasionally, until tender, 3 to 6 minutes. Add the garlic, sage, pepper flakes, ½ teaspoon salt, and a few grinds of black pepper and cook for 1 minute, until fragrant. Add the wine and cook, scraping any browned bits from the bottom of the pan, until most of the liquid has evaporated. Add the kale, and cook, tossing often, until wilted and tender, about 2 minutes. Off the heat, stir in the brown rice.

4. Scoop the cooked squash from the shells, leaving about a ¼-inch border around the edges to help the squash keep its shape, and add to the skillet. Season with 1 teaspoon salt and a few grinds of black pepper and mix well. By this point the mixture should be fairly cool. If not, set aside for 10 minutes until cool.

5. In a small bowl, mix together the Fontina and pecorino. Add half the cheese to the squash mixture and toss well. Spoon the mixture back into the squash shells, dividing it evenly among them. Sprinkle the remaining cheese over the squash.

6. Return to the oven and bake until they are heated through and the cheese is lightly browned, 15 to 20 minutes.

7. Top the squash with freshly grated nutmeg, if using, and serve hot.

Spaghetti with Sweet Corn Pesto

SERVES 4 TO 6

7 tablespoons extra-virgin olive oil, divided

½ cup panko bread crumbs

¼ teaspoon crushed red pepper flakes

Kosher salt and freshly ground black pepper

4 cups fresh corn kernels cut (from 5 to 7 ears of corn)

2 garlic cloves, smashed and peeled

½ cup grated Parmesan cheese

1 pound spaghetti

2 pints cherry tomatoes, cut in half through the stem

1 cup fresh basil leaves, torn into pieces, divided

Grated lemon zest, for serving (optional)

GET AHEAD

The spicy bread crumbs will keep for several days in a sealed container, and you can make the corn pesto a few hours in advance. You may just need to add additional pasta water when reheating the sauce.

When I started writing this book, I knew there was one recipe that had to make the cut. This spaghetti was one of the first recipes I ever published on my website, and to this day it's by far the recipe I hear about the most from friends, family, and readers online.

With fresh corn, cherry tomatoes, and basil, this pasta is a celebration of all things summer, but it's the corn "pesto"—a sauce made with sautéed corn, garlic, Parmesan, and olive oil—that really makes it special. It's sweet, creamy, and savory with a flavor truly all its own.

This recipe epitomizes the kind of food I like to make—it's colorful, fun to eat, and a little bit unexpected. And while it may use more pans and equipment than my average recipe, when you want to make a serious summer crowd-pleaser, it's worth every minute.

1. In a large (12-inch) skillet, heat 1 tablespoon of the olive oil over medium heat. Add the panko, pepper flakes, and ¼ teaspoon salt. Cook, tossing often, until the panko is golden brown, 3 to 5 minutes, then transfer to a small bowl to cool.

2. Bring a large pot of salted water to a boil for the pasta.

3. Meanwhile, carefully wipe out the skillet with a paper towel. Turn the heat to medium and add 3 tablespoons of the olive oil. Add the corn, garlic, and 1 teaspoon salt and cook, stirring occasionally, until the corn is tender and the garlic is beginning to soften, 4 to 6 minutes. Let cool for 10 minutes. Measure out ½ cup of the corn kernels and set aside.

4. Transfer the rest of the corn and the garlic to a food processor. Add 1½ teaspoons salt and ½ teaspoon pepper and process until coarsely pureed. With the machine running, pour in the remaining 3 tablespoons olive oil and process until smooth. Add the Parmesan and pulse until just combined. Set aside. (Or refrigerate for up to 3 hours before using.)

5. Add the spaghetti to the pot of boiling water and cook until just al dente according to the package directions. Reserving 1 cup of the pasta water, drain the pasta in a colander and set aside. Working quickly, transfer the corn pesto to the pasta pot, along with ½ cup of the reserved pasta water. Bring to a simmer over medium-low heat, stirring until the pesto loosens and the sauce comes together.

6. Off the heat, return the pasta to the pot, along with the tomatoes, reserved corn kernels, and half the basil leaves. Toss well with tongs, and if the pasta seems dry, add another splash of pasta water.

7. Transfer the pasta to a serving bowl and top with the remaining basil, lemon zest (if using), and half of the bread crumbs. Serve in shallow bowls, passing the rest of the bread crumbs around the table in a small bowl.

Red Curry Lentils
with Sweet Potatoes & Spinach

SERVES 4

3 tablespoons extra-virgin olive oil, divided

1 pound sweet potatoes, peeled and ¾-inch diced (about 2 medium potatoes)

1 medium yellow onion, chopped

1 tablespoon minced garlic (2 large cloves)

1 tablespoon grated fresh ginger (about a 1-inch knob)

3 tablespoons Thai red curry paste

1 small chile pepper, such as Fresno or serrano, seeded and minced

1 teaspoon ground turmeric

1 cup red lentils, rinsed

4 cups (1 quart) low-sodium vegetable broth

2 teaspoons kosher salt, plus more to taste

1 (13-ounce) can full-fat coconut milk

1 (4- to 5-ounce) bag baby spinach

Juice of half a lime

Cooked rice, for serving (optional)

Fresh cilantro leaves, for serving

Toasted unsweetened coconut flakes, for serving (optional)

Inspired by the flavors of Thai red curry and Indian masoor dal, this veggie-packed weeknight wonder is a recipe I created for the *New York Times*. It delivers on the richness of a Thai curry and the comfort of a spiced Indian dal, with minimal effort and just a bit of simmering and stirring (preferably done while having a glass of wine). This is a healthy, hearty dinner that I make at least once a month.

1. In a medium Dutch oven or other heavy-bottomed pot, heat 2 tablespoons of the olive oil over medium-high heat. Add the sweet potatoes and cook, tossing occasionally, until they are browned all over, 5 to 7 minutes (they will not be completely cooked). Transfer the potatoes to a plate and set aside.

2. Add the remaining 1 tablespoon olive oil to the pot and reduce the heat to medium-low. Add the onion and cook, stirring occasionally, until translucent, 4 to 6 minutes. Add the garlic, ginger, red curry paste, chile, and turmeric and cook for 1 minute, until fragrant.

3. Add the lentils, vegetable broth, salt, and reserved sweet potatoes and bring to a boil. Reduce the heat and simmer, uncovered and stirring occasionally, until the lentils are just tender, 20 to 25 minutes.

4. Add the coconut milk and simmer, stirring occasionally, until the liquid has reduced and the lentils are creamy and falling apart, 15 to 20 more minutes.

5. Add the spinach and cook, tossing often, until just wilted, 2 to 3 minutes. Off the heat, stir in the lime juice and taste for seasonings, adding more salt if needed.

6. Serve in shallow bowls, over rice, if using. Garnish with cilantro and toasted coconut, if using.

LEFTOVERS FOR LUNCH
If you want to plan ahead, make a double batch to have leftovers for lunch all week.

Crispy Cauliflower & Chickpea Cakes with Moroccan Spices

SERVES 4

1 medium head cauliflower (about 2 pounds)

1 small yellow onion, sliced crosswise into ½-inch-thick rings (about 1 heaping cup)

3 tablespoons extra-virgin olive oil

Kosher salt and freshly ground black pepper

1 (15-ounce) can chickpeas, rinsed and drained

2 medium garlic cloves, coarsely chopped

4 tablespoons mild or spicy harissa sauce, divided, plus more for serving (see Tip, page 145)

3 tablespoons chopped fresh parsley

2 teaspoons light brown sugar

1 teaspoon sweet paprika

½ teaspoon ground cumin

½ teaspoon ground ginger

¼ teaspoon ground cinnamon

1 cup chickpea flour, divided

Neutral oil, such as canola or grapeseed, for pan-frying

1 cup plain whole-milk yogurt, seasoned with ¼ teaspoon salt, for serving

One very real challenge of cooking in real life is juggling the various food restrictions, allergies, and preferences of the people in our lives. We want to make something delicious that everyone can eat, and more important, that everyone will like, and that can be hard when whole categories of food are off the table.

While I can't promise this recipe will work for every single diet, it does cover a majority of common "-frees." It's gluten-free, egg-free, nut-free, and both dairy-free and vegan if you serve it with a plant-based yogurt. And beyond all of those qualifications, these cauliflower and chickpea cakes are just plain delicious! Made with lots of Moroccan spices and harissa, they have smoky flavor and just a touch of heat. They get a nice crisp edge when pan-fried, while the inside stays tender and moist.

I like to serve the cakes with extra harissa on the side for dipping, and lightly salted yogurt for a touch of creaminess. These would also be fun as an appetizer, formed into tiny balls instead of cakes.

1. Preheat the oven to 400°F.

2. Cut the cauliflower into 1-inch florets and place them on a sheet pan. Add the onion rings and drizzle with the olive oil. Sprinkle with 1 teaspoon salt and toss well. Roast until tender and lightly browned, 30 to 35 minutes, tossing twice throughout. Set aside until cool.

3. In a food processor, combine the chickpeas, garlic, and 3 tablespoons of the harissa and process until coarsely pureed. Transfer to a large bowl.

4. Add the roasted cauliflower and onion to the food processor and process until very finely chopped or "riced," but not pureed. Add to the bowl with the chickpeas.

5. To the chickpea and cauliflower mixture, add the remaining 1 tablespoon harissa, the parsley, brown sugar, paprika, cumin, ginger, cinnamon, 1 teaspoon salt, and a few grinds of black pepper. Mix well. Add ½ cup of the chickpea flour and mix until smooth.

6. Place the remaining ½ cup chickpea flour on a flat plate. Use a ⅓-cup measure to scoop portions of the cauliflower-chickpea mixture and form into patties about 1 inch thick. Gently dip the patties into the chickpea flour until coated on both sides, reshaping if necessary, and place them on a plate.

RECIPE CONTINUES ON PAGE 145

7. Line a plate with paper towels and have at the ready. Heat a 12-inch skillet over medium-high heat. Add 3 tablespoons canola oil and when the oil is hot (a crumb dropped into the oil should immediately begin to sizzle), add 3 of the cakes. Fry, pressing down gently but firmly with a spatula until the cakes are about ½ inch thick, until golden brown on the bottom, 1 to 2 minutes. Flip and cook for 1 to 2 minutes until golden brown on the other side. Transfer to the paper towels to drain and sprinkle with salt.

8. Repeat with the remaining cakes in batches, adding more oil as necessary. Serve hot with more harissa and salted yogurt on the side.

TIP

Harissa is a North African red pepper sauce. It's sweet and smoky with a ranging amount of heat. Either mild or spicy harissa will work here—just make sure to buy harissa *sauce*, not harissa *paste*.

GET AHEAD

This recipe has a few different steps, but you can do any number of them in advance. You can roast the cauliflower and onions, make the mixture for the cakes, and even shape the cakes themselves. If you plan to do the latter in advance, store the shaped cakes on a parchment lined tray in the fridge for up to 12 hours, covered with plastic wrap.

LEFTOVERS FOR LUNCH

I often make a double batch of these cakes to have leftovers on hand for a quick and healthy lunch. I freeze the leftover (cooked) cakes on a plate, then transfer them to freezer bags. I reheat them on a sheet pan at 350 degrees for 15 to 20 minutes, or until heated through.

On the Side

Side of Greens with Garlic & Soy 150

Maple-Roasted Squash with Grapes, Shallots & Rosemary 153

Warm Herbed Farro 154

Green Beans with Crispy Capers & Garlic 157

Braised Green Cabbage with Bacon & Caraway Seeds 158

Crunchy Cucumber Salad with Peanuts & Chili Flakes 161

Creamy Polenta 162

Asparagus Vinaigrette 165

Roasted Cauliflower with Fried Sage & Hazelnuts 166

White Rice with Ginger & Leeks 169

Perfect Picnic Coleslaw 170

Roasted Broccolini with Pickled Pepperoncini 173

Potato and Chickpea Salad with Dill & Cornichons 174

Spiced Sweet Potatoes with Pecans & Pomegranate Seeds 177

Grilled Zucchini with Charred Lemon Dressing, Feta & Mint 178

Crispy Smashed Potatoes with Salsa Verde 181

Coconut Creamed Corn 182

Brussels Sprouts with Dates & Crispy Prosciutto 185

Side of Greens
with Garlic & Soy

SERVES 2 TO 4

1 pound kale, Swiss chard, collard greens, or a combination (2 medium bunches)

3 tablespoons extra-virgin olive oil

2 medium garlic cloves, minced

Pinch of crushed red pepper flakes

½ teaspoon kosher salt

½ teaspoon soy sauce or tamari

Let's start with the basics here—the simplest, most delicious method for cooking leafy greens. Blanching and sautéing greens takes barely 10 minutes and is the perfect way to use up that bunch of kale you optimistically brought home from the grocery store and still haven't touched.

The seasonings here—a bit of garlic, soy sauce, and red pepper flakes—are just enough to give the greens a hint of salt and umami, but a sprinkle of sesame seeds, sliced scallions, or a squeeze of lemon would all be nice additions depending on what else you're having. As is, these greens are versatile enough to go with just about anything.

The serving size here is really a suggestion—every bunch of greens is a different size, and I could easily take down a whole skillet of greens myself. If you want to double or triple the recipe, go for it! Just sauté the greens in batches to avoid crowding the pan.

1. Bring a large pot of water to a boil.

2. Meanwhile, prep the greens: Trim and discard any tough stems or ribs that are ¼ inch or thicker. Coarsely chop the greens and rinse them thoroughly in a colander, working in batches if necessary.

3. Add the greens to the boiling water and cook, stirring occasionally, until all the greens are wilted, 2 to 3 minutes. Using tongs, return the greens to the colander to drain.

4. In a 12-inch skillet, heat the olive oil, garlic, and pepper flakes over medium-low heat. Cook, tossing often, until the garlic is pale golden and fragrant, 1 to 2 minutes.

5. Add the greens and salt and cook, tossing to coat the greens in the oil. Cook, tossing often, until tender, 3 to 5 minutes. Off the heat, add the soy sauce and toss.

6. Transfer the greens to a serving bowl and serve hot, warm, or at room temperature.

Maple-Roasted Squash
with Grapes, Shallots & Rosemary

SERVES 4

2 small delicata squash (about 1½ pounds total)

1½ cups seedless red grapes, stems removed

3 medium shallots, sliced ¼-inch thick

2 fresh rosemary sprigs

3 tablespoons extra-virgin olive oil

Kosher salt and freshly ground black pepper

1 tablespoon maple syrup

1 tablespoon apple cider vinegar

I used to roast a lot of butternut squash, but I've recently become a delicata squash convert. The skin is tender enough that you don't have to peel it, and I love how the delicata's cylindrical shape makes for perfect little half-moon slices. Here, I'm roasting them along with red grapes, shallots, and rosemary for a sheet pan side dish full of fall flavor and deliciously contrasting textures. The squash caramelizes beautifully as it roasts, the shallots get nice and crispy, and the grapes become soft and juicy. A final drizzle of maple syrup and vinegar releases all the tasty browned bits from the pan.

Serve this squash alongside a roast chicken, with some sausages, or as part of a veggie-and-grain bowl.

1. Preheat the oven to 425°F.

2. Cut the delicata squash in half lengthwise, scoop out the seeds, and slice crosswise into ½-inch-thick half-moons. Place on a sheet pan, along with the grapes, shallots, and rosemary.

3. Drizzle with the olive oil and sprinkle with ½ teaspoon salt and a few grinds of black pepper. Toss well and spread into an even layer. Roast for 30 minutes, tossing once halfway through.

4. Drizzle the maple syrup over the vegetables and toss. Return to the oven until the squash is nicely caramelized, about 5 minutes. Immediately add the vinegar to the pan and toss, scraping up any browned bits from the pan.

5. Sprinkle with salt, transfer to a serving dish, and serve warm or at room temperature.

SIMPLE SWAP

If you can't find delicata squash, you can use butternut squash instead. (And for the record, I still love butternut squash!) Use 1½ pounds precubed butternut squash, or peel and seed a small (2-pound) squash, and cut it into 1-inch cubes. Butternut squash may need a few more minutes in the oven, so just keep an eye on it and test for doneness with a fork.

Warm Herbed Farro

SERVES 6 TO 8

3 tablespoons unsalted butter
or extra-virgin olive oil

1 large yellow onion, chopped
(about 1½ cups)

1½ teaspoons chopped fresh
thyme leaves

4 cups (1 quart) low-sodium
chicken or vegetable broth

2 cups whole-grain farro,
rinsed

Kosher salt and freshly ground
black pepper

⅓ cup chopped fresh parsley

⅓ cup minced scallions (2 to
3 scallions)

Growing up, we had rice pilaf a lot. It came in a box with a little seasoning packet and seemed to go with just about everything my mom made. This is my updated version, with farro instead of rice, and chicken broth and fresh herbs in place of the flavor packet. It's warm and comforting and slightly creamy in texture, almost like a risotto without all the stirring. Even my mom agrees it gives rice in the box a serious run for its money.

1. In a large saucepan, heat the butter over medium-low heat. Add the onion and thyme and cook, stirring occasionally, until the onion is translucent, 6 to 8 minutes.

2. Stir in the broth, farro, 2 teaspoons salt, and ½ teaspoon pepper and bring to a boil over medium-high heat. Reduce the heat, cover, and simmer until the farro is al dente, 35 to 40 minutes. (There will still be some liquid in the pot at this point.)

3. Add the parsley and scallions and simmer uncovered, stirring occasionally, until the farro is tender and all the liquid has been absorbed, 5 to 10 more minutes. Taste for seasonings and serve warm.

MAKE IT A MEAL
Add some rotisserie chicken and a handful of salad greens or roasted veggies for comforting weeknight dinner.

Green Beans
with Crispy Capers & Garlic

SERVES 4

Kosher salt

1 pound green beans or
haricots verts, trimmed

2 tablespoons extra-virgin
olive oil

3 tablespoons capers, drained
and patted dry

1 tablespoon chopped garlic

Juice of half a lemon, for
serving

These garlicky, lemony green beans pack a ton of flavor for a dish with so few ingredients. Fried capers add a nice salty crunch (you'll want to sprinkle them on everything!) and a touch of vinegar gives the beans an addictive quality. That's more than I can say about most green beans. I think of these as an everyday side dish, but they'd also be a fresh alternative to Thanksgiving green bean casserole.

1. Bring a large pot of salted water to a boil and place a large bowl of ice water next to the stove. When the water comes to a boil, add the green beans and cook until bright green and crisp-tender, 2 to 5 minutes.

2. Using tongs, lift the green beans from the boiling water and immediately add them to the bowl of ice water. When the beans are cool, drain and pat them dry with a clean kitchen towel.

3. Line a small plate with paper towels. Heat a large skillet over medium-high heat. Drizzle in the oil and when the oil is hot, add the capers and cook, tossing occasionally until crispy and lightly browned, about 2 minutes. Using a slotted spoon, transfer the capers to the paper towels.

4. Reduce the heat under the skillet to medium. Add the garlic, green beans, and ½ teaspoon salt. Cook, tossing often, until the beans are heated through and the garlic is tender, about 2 minutes, reducing the heat if the garlic begins to brown.

5. Transfer the beans to a serving platter and squeeze the lemon over them. Spoon the fried capers on top and serve hot or warm.

Braised Green Cabbage
with Bacon & Caraway Seeds

SERVES 6

4 slices bacon, cut into ½-inch pieces

1 teaspoon caraway seeds

½ cup apple cider or apple juice

Half a large head green cabbage, cored and thinly sliced (about 10 cups)

Kosher salt and freshly ground black pepper

1 crisp apple, such as Fuji, cored and thinly sliced

2 tablespoons apple cider vinegar

Cabbage is a truly underrated vegetable. It always looks kind of sad to me at the grocery store—sitting there in the pre-shredded salad kits or watching people pass by when they realize it isn't a head of cauliflower. But just think of all the different ways there are to eat cabbage: It can be steamed, sautéed, charred, caramelized, fermented, shredded, or braised, to name a few!

Of all the delicious ways to prepare cabbage, my very favorite is to slice it thinly and cook it in bacon fat, with a splash of fresh apple cider and a sprinkle of caraway seeds for a hint of rye flavor. This is a great side dish with any hearty fall or winter meal, but I particularly like it with pork or chicken sausages.

1. Line a small plate with a paper towel. In a 12-inch skillet, cook the bacon over medium heat, tossing often, until browned and crisp, 5 to 7 minutes. Transfer the bacon to the paper towel and set aside.

2. Add the caraway seeds to the skillet and cook for 30 seconds over medium heat, until fragrant. Slowly pour in the cider (careful, it might splatter!), and bring to a simmer over medium-high heat, scraping any browned bits from the pan. Add half of the cabbage, 1 teaspoon salt, and a few grinds of black pepper and cook, tossing often, until the cabbage has wilted.

3. Add the rest of the cabbage and the apples. Cook over medium heat, tossing occasionally, until the cabbage is tender and browned in some spots, 15 to 20 minutes.

4. Off the heat, add the vinegar and toss, scraping any browned bits from the pan. Add the reserved bacon, taste for seasonings, and serve.

MAKE IT A MEAL
Add a poached or fried egg and some toast for a delicious breakfast or lunch.

Crunchy Cucumber Salad with Peanuts & Chili Flakes

SERVES 6 TO 8

2 pounds Persian or other small seedless cucumbers

1 teaspoon kosher salt

2 tablespoons toasted sesame oil

2 tablespoons seasoned rice vinegar

1 tablespoon peanut or grapeseed oil

2 teaspoons soy sauce or tamari

1 teaspoon sugar

¼ teaspoon crushed red pepper flakes

⅓ cup lightly salted roasted peanuts, very finely chopped

Chopped fresh cilantro, for serving (optional)

This simple cucumber salad is loosely inspired by *pai huang gua*, a Sichuan dish of smashed cucumbers dressed with sesame oil and dried chiles. Instead of smashing the cucumbers, I like to use small seedless cucumbers, cutting them into little coins that stay crisp even as the salad sits. This salad is delicious and super refreshing on a hot summer day, but most often I make it alongside the Salmon with Honey & Chili Crunch (page 122) for a spicy weeknight dinner that leans heavily on pantry staples.

1. Slice the cucumbers about ¼-inch thick and place them in a colander set over the sink. Add the salt and toss. Set aside for 30 minutes, tossing occasionally. Gently pat the cucumbers with a paper towel to absorb more of the liquid.

2. Meanwhile, in a large bowl, combine the sesame oil, rice vinegar, peanut oil, soy sauce, sugar, and pepper flakes and whisk vigorously until smooth.

3. Add the cucumbers to the bowl and toss well. Just before serving, add the peanuts and toss again. Garnish with cilantro, if using. Serve immediately or store covered in the refrigerator for up to 24 hours.

Creamy Polenta

SERVES 4 TO 6

2 teaspoons kosher salt, plus more to taste

1 cup stone-ground or medium-grind yellow cornmeal

½ cup whole milk

3 tablespoons unsalted butter

¾ cup grated Grana Padano or Parmesan cheese (2½ ounces)

Freshly ground black pepper

This is the classic soft polenta that I like to serve with my One-Pan Chicken Meatballs with Red Sauce & Spinach (page 84), Braised Short Ribs with Port, Shallots & Cranberries (page 111), or even on its own with a pile of steamed greens on top. The trick to making creamy, nonlumpy polenta, is adding the cornmeal slowly, whisking the entire time. It's a two-hander, just for those few seconds. Polenta will thicken considerably as it sits, so if you need to reheat it, add a splash of water and milk, and warm it over low heat, stirring often.

1. In a large saucepan, combine 5 cups of water and salt and bring to a boil over medium-high heat. Whisking constantly, gradually sprinkle in the cornmeal. Once all the cornmeal has been added, continue whisking constantly for about 1 minute, until the polenta begins to thicken.

2. Reduce the heat to low and simmer uncovered, stirring and scraping the sides and bottom of the pot occasionally, until the polenta is very thick, about 25 minutes.

3. Add the milk and butter, return to a simmer, and cook, stirring occasionally, until the polenta is thick again, 5 to 10 more minutes.

4. Off the heat, stir in the cheese. Add a few grinds of black pepper and more salt to taste, and set aside for 10 minutes before serving, until slightly set. The polenta will continue to thicken as it cools. To reheat, add a splash of water and milk and heat the polenta, covered, over low heat.

MAKE IT A MEAL
Of course, polenta is a wonderful accompaniment to lots of different main dishes, but it's also a delicious base for roasted veggies or sautéed greens. Try it with a fried egg for a comforting breakfast or weeknight dinner.

Asparagus Vinaigrette

1 pound asparagus

4 tablespoons extra-virgin olive oil, divided

Kosher salt and freshly ground black pepper

1 tablespoon minced shallot

2 teaspoons red wine vinegar

½ teaspoon whole-grain mustard

1 tablespoon minced fresh parsley

Pinch of granulated sugar

Poireaux vinaigrette is a classic French bistro dish of slow-roasted leeks marinated in a mustard vinaigrette. It's simple, elegant, and very French. In this recipe, I'm giving asparagus the "leeks vinaigrette treatment": I roast the asparagus spears until just tender and then drizzle them with a tangy red wine vinegar and mustard vinaigrette.

This is an ideal dish for entertaining because, as with leeks vinaigrette, the asparagus is best made in advance and served at room temperature. If possible, avoid super-skinny asparagus spears when making this recipe; slightly thicker stalks will hold up better as they roast.

1. Preheat the oven to 375°F.

2. Trim 1 inch from the bottom of the asparagus spears and discard. Place the asparagus on a sheet pan, drizzle with 2 tablespoons of the olive oil, and toss. Sprinkle with ¼ teaspoon salt and roast until crisp-tender and just starting to take on color, 14 to 22 minutes, depending on the thickness of the asparagus.

3. Meanwhile, in a small bowl, whisk together the remaining 2 tablespoons olive oil, the shallot, vinegar, mustard, parsley, sugar, ¼ teaspoon salt, and a few grinds of black pepper.

4. Transfer the hot asparagus to a rimmed serving dish just large enough to hold it. Pour the dressing over the asparagus and set aside until warm or room temperature before serving.

COOKING FOR A CROWD
This is an easy side to scale up for a larger group. If you're doubling or tripling the recipe, roast the asparagus in batches to avoid crowding, then arrange it all on a platter and top with the vinaigrette.

Roasted Cauliflower
with Fried Sage & Hazelnuts

SERVES 4

1 large head cauliflower (about 2½ pounds)

3 tablespoons extra-virgin olive oil

Kosher salt and freshly ground black pepper

3 tablespoons unsalted butter

⅓ cup packed fresh sage leaves

⅓ cup whole raw hazelnuts, chopped

Freshly grated nutmeg, for serving

This recipe illustrates how easy it is to transform a pan of plain roasted vegetables into a delicious, composed dish, with just a few additional ingredients and very little effort. Roasted cauliflower is great on its own, but tossed with hazelnuts and brown butter–fried sage, it's a side dish that just might steal the show. Don't skip out on the freshly grated nutmeg if you can help it. It gives the cauliflower the most incredible, nutty aroma.

1. Preheat the oven to 425°F.

2. Cut the cauliflower into 2-inch florets. Place the cauliflower on a sheet pan, drizzle with the olive oil, sprinkle with ½ teaspoon salt, and a few grinds of black pepper. Toss well.

3. Roast the cauliflower until tender and browned, 25 to 30 minutes, tossing once halfway through. Transfer to a serving dish large enough to hold it in one layer.

4. In a small skillet, melt the butter over medium heat. When the butter begins to sizzle, add the sage and hazelnuts. Cook, tossing often, until the butter is nutty and fragrant and the nuts are lightly toasted, about 3 minutes. Remove from the heat.

5. Spoon the fried hazelnuts and sage over the cauliflower, gently breaking up the sage leaves with a serving spoon. Sprinkle lightly with salt and freshly grated nutmeg and serve.

White Rice
with Ginger & Leeks

SERVES 4 TO 6

3 tablespoons extra-virgin olive oil, divided

2 tablespoons minced, peeled fresh ginger (from a 2-inch knob)

1½ cups long- or medium-grain white rice, rinsed until the water runs clear

Kosher salt

1 medium leek, trimmed

Grated zest of half a lime (optional), for serving

I often make a pot of white or brown rice to have with dinner, but plain rice never feels exciting enough when I'm having friends over. When a little pizzazz is in order, I make this recipe. Fresh ginger is used in so many cuisines and flavor profiles around the world, and it makes this rice a bit of a chameleon. It goes well with pretty much any meat or fish. I make it most often with roast chicken (see page 106), white fish (see page 121), and salmon (see page 122). A sprinkle of lime zest makes a nice, fragrant garnish, but isn't necessary if you don't have a lime on hand.

1. In a large saucepan, heat 1 tablespoon of the olive oil over medium heat. Add the ginger and cook until fragrant but not browned, about 30 seconds. Add the rice and 1 teaspoon salt and stir to coat the grains. Add 2½ cups water and bring to a boil over medium-high heat. Stir, reduce the heat to low, cover, and simmer for 15 minutes. Set aside off the heat, covered, for 10 minutes, then fluff the rice with a fork.

2. Meanwhile, halve the leek in lengthwise and thinly slice crosswise into half-moons. Rinse well, then pat the leeks dry with a kitchen towel. In a 10-inch skillet, heat the remaining 2 tablespoons oil over medium-low heat. Add the leeks and ¼ teaspoon salt and cook tossing occasionally, until tender but not browned, 7 to 10 minutes.

3. Add the leeks to the fluffed rice and mix gently. Taste and add salt as necessary. Transfer to a serving dish, garnish with lime zest, if using, and serve warm or at room temperature.

Perfect Picnic Coleslaw

1 small head green cabbage
(2½ pounds)

Kosher salt and freshly ground
black pepper

2 cups julienned Tuscan/
lacinato or curly kale

1 cup grated carrots (about
2 medium carrots)

¾ cup thinly sliced scallions
(about 4 scallions)

½ cup mayonnaise

3 tablespoons seasoned rice
vinegar (see Tip)

1 teaspoon Dijon mustard

This one is for my friend Julia, who has been like a sister to me since we were assigned to be roommates our first year of college. She *loves* coleslaw. So much so, that it was even her go-to hangover food, which still baffles me. According to Julia, a good coleslaw should have lots of crunch (a soggy coleslaw is a sad coleslaw) and the dressing should strike a perfect balance between mayo and vinegar. That's what I'm going for here—a creamy dressing flavored with tangy rice vinegar and mustard—and plenty of crunchy veggies. I like to serve this slaw on my Spicy Barbecue Pulled Chicken Sandwiches (page 96) and as part of cookout spreads all summer long.

1. Halve and core the cabbage. Using a mandoline or a sharp knife, slice the cabbage crosswise into thin shreds (you should have about 10 cups) and place in a very large bowl. Add 1 teaspoon salt and massage for 30 seconds, until the cabbage has wilted slightly.

2. Add the kale, carrots, and scallions and toss.

3. In a large glass measuring cup, whisk together the mayonnaise, vinegar, mustard, 1 teaspoon salt, and ½ teaspoon black pepper. Pour the dressing over the vegetables and toss well with tongs.

4. Season to taste with salt and pepper and serve at room temperature.

TIP

This recipe calls for seasoned rice vinegar, which is flavored with a bit of sugar and salt. If you have only regular rice vinegar, add a pinch of granulated sugar to your dressing.

Roasted Broccolini
with Pickled Pepperoncini

SERVES 4 TO 6

1½ pounds broccolini (3 to 4 bunches)

3 tablespoons extra-virgin olive oil

Kosher salt

⅓ cup coarsely chopped jarred pepperoncini (stems removed)

¼ cup chopped fresh flat-leaf parsley

1 tablespoon red wine vinegar

A recipe that rhymes! This roasted broccolini is exactly what I want to eat alongside cheesy or saucy dishes—the perfect little something green and bright between bites of pizza or pasta. Pickled pepperoncini are vinegary baby peppers. They're little flavor bombs, and I like to keep a jar in the fridge to add instant personality to any simple roasted vegetable, sandwich, or chopped salad.

1. Preheat the oven to 400°F.

2. Trim 1 inch from the broccolini stems and cut any large stalks in half lengthwise so the pieces are all roughly the same thickness. Place the broccolini on a sheet pan and drizzle with the olive oil. Toss well with your hands, then spread the broccolini into an even layer and sprinkle with ½ teaspoon salt.

3. Roast until tender, 15 to 25 minutes, tossing once halfway through.

4. Meanwhile, in a small bowl, combine the pepperoncini, parsley, and vinegar. Add a pinch of salt, toss, and set aside.

5. When the broccolini is tender, transfer to a serving dish. Spoon the pepperoncini mixture on top, along with any juices left in the bowl. Sprinkle with salt and serve warm or at room temperature.

SIMPLE SWAP

If regular broccoli is what happens to be in your fridge, that works here, too! Just be sure to cut the broccoli into similarly sized florets so it cooks evenly.

Potato and Chickpea Salad with Dill & Cornichons

1½ pounds small red or baby Yukon Gold potatoes

Kosher salt

¼ cup extra-virgin olive oil

1 tablespoon champagne vinegar or white wine vinegar

½ teaspoon Dijon mustard

Freshly ground black pepper

1 (15-ounce) can chickpeas, rinsed and drained

½ cup minced red onion (half a small onion)

¾ cup cornichons, finely chopped (about 3.5 ounces)

2 tablespoons mayonnaise

⅓ cup minced fresh dill

While I love dreaming up new recipe ideas, I still tend to gravitate to beloved, nostalgic foods, especially when I'm cooking for other people. My hunch is I'm not alone. Familiar foods are comforting, and they've stood the test of time for a reason. But that doesn't mean there isn't room to find ways to make classic dishes feel current and fresh.

Take this potato salad, for example. It's got the hallmarks of a retro potato salad—mayonnaise, minced red onion, and dill—along with a can of chickpeas to lighten things up and diced cornichons for a vinegary crunch in each bite. It's proof that with a few updates, a good potato salad (and a jar of pickles) never goes out of style.

1. Place the potatoes in a large pot and add 2 tablespoons salt and enough water to cover generously. Bring to a boil over high heat and cook until the potatoes are tender when pierced with a fork, 15 to 20 minutes, depending on the size of the potatoes. Drain and set aside until just cool enough to handle.

2. Meanwhile, in a large bowl, combine the olive oil, vinegar, mustard, ½ teaspoon salt, and ¼ teaspoon black pepper and whisk until smooth. Stir in the chickpeas and onion and set aside.

3. When the potatoes are just cool enough to handle, cut them in half (or quarters if they are larger than 1½ inches in diameter) and add to the bowl with the dressing. Toss gently and set aside, tossing occasionally, until cool.

4. Add the cornichons and mayonnaise to the potatoes and mix well. Add the dill and toss again. Season with more salt and black pepper to taste. Serve at room temperature.

Spiced Sweet Potatoes
with Pecans & Pomegranate Seeds

SERVES 4 TO 6

2½ pounds sweet potatoes
(3 to 4 medium potatoes)

2 fresh rosemary sprigs

4 tablespoons extra-virgin
olive oil

½ teaspoon ground cinnamon

½ teaspoon chipotle chile
powder

Kosher salt and freshly ground
black pepper

¾ cup pecans, coarsely
chopped

2 tablespoons maple syrup

⅓ cup pomegranate arils

These are my fancy sweet potatoes. Instead of roasting them with some salt and a drizzle of olive oil as I usually do, I add some cinnamon, chipotle chile powder, and fresh rosemary to the mix. The chipotle powder gives the potatoes just a hint of smoky heat, and the rosemary and cinnamon warm everything up with a fragrant aroma.

Just before the potatoes are tender, I add a handful of chopped pecans and a splash of maple syrup to the pan. The maple syrup helps caramelize the potatoes and coats the nuts as they toast. And finally, I sprinkle pomegranate seeds over the potatoes for a gorgeous pop of color and a juicy crunch in each bite. The result is a dish that feels festive, complete, and worthy of any holiday feast—but this recipe is too easy and too good to save for special occasions!

1. Preheat the oven to 425°F.

2. Peel the sweet potatoes and dice them into 1-inch pieces. Place them on a sheet pan along with the rosemary sprigs.

3. In a small bowl, whisk together the olive oil, cinnamon, chipotle powder, 1 teaspoon salt, and ¼ teaspoon black pepper. Pour the mixture over the sweet potatoes and toss well.

4. Roast the potatoes until almost tender, 20 to 25 minutes, tossing once halfway through.

5. Add the pecans and maple syrup and toss well. Roast until the potatoes are tender when pierced with a fork, 5 to 10 more minutes.

6. Discard the rosemary stems, add the pomegranate arils to the sheet pan and toss. Spoon the potatoes into a serving bowl and serve warm or at room temperature.

COOKING FOR A CROWD

If you want to double this recipe, spread the potatoes across 2 sheet pans to avoid crowding them.

Grilled Zucchini
with Charred Lemon Dressing, Feta & Mint

SERVES 6

4 small-ish zucchini (6 to 8 inches long)

4 tablespoons extra-virgin olive oil, divided, plus more for drizzling

Kosher salt and freshly ground black pepper

Half a lemon

½ teaspoon honey

⅛ teaspoon ground cumin

3 ounces feta cheese, crumbled

A small handful of fresh mint leaves

Zucchini planks are one of my go-to grilled veggies, because they're big enough to grill without falling through the grates, and because they really benefit from a little bit of char-grilled flavor. I'm giving the grill even more action here, by making a dressing with charred lemon. It's smoky, a little sweet, and a true delight poured over the hot zucchini. Add some diced feta and a few mint leaves, and you've got a perfect summer side ready to go before the meat even comes off the grill.

1. Heat a grill to medium-high heat.

2. Slice the zucchini lengthwise into ½-inch-thick planks and spread them on a sheet pan. Drizzle them all over with 2 tablespoons of the olive oil and toss to coat. Season the zucchini with ½ teaspoon salt and a few grinds of black pepper, then flip and repeat on the other side.

3. Grill the zucchini for 3 to 5 minutes on each side, until the zucchini is just tender and has nice grill marks on both sides, 3 to 5 minutes per side. While the zucchini is grilling, drizzle a little olive oil over the lemon half. Place it on the grill, cut-side down, and grill until golden brown and charred on the cut side, about 3 minutes. Set aside until cool enough to handle.

4. Transfer the grilled zucchini to a large serving platter. Squeeze the lemon half into a small bowl and discard any seeds. Add the remaining 2 tablespoons olive oil, the honey, cumin, and ¼ teaspoon salt and whisk vigorously until smooth.

5. Pour the dressing over the hot zucchini, then top with the feta. Tear the mint leaves into pieces and scatter them over the zucchini, finish with a few grinds of black pepper, and serve warm or at room temperature.

COOKING FOR A CROWD
This recipe doubles easily and looks beautiful served on a long platter.

TIP
Bigger isn't always better. I look for zucchini on the smaller side, even in the height of summer. Smaller zucchini and summer squash tend to be more flavorful and less watery than huge ones.

Crispy Smashed Potatoes with Salsa Verde

SERVES 4

2 pounds small Yukon Gold potatoes (about 1½ inches in diameter)

Kosher salt and freshly ground black pepper

6 tablespoons extra-virgin olive oil, divided

3 tablespoons chopped fresh parsley

2 tablespoons chopped fresh mint leaves

2 tablespoons capers, drained and coarsely chopped

2 tablespoons chopped scallion (about 1 scallion)

1 garlic clove, minced

2 tablespoons red wine vinegar or sherry vinegar

While smashed potatoes may look like a fancy restaurant dish, they're actually easy (and fun!) to make at home. The potatoes get boiled until just tender, then smashed and roasted with lots of olive oil until all those craggy edges are crispy and golden brown. The finishing touch here is a Spanish-inspired salsa verde, made with a pile of green herbs, capers, and garlic. It's the perfect vinegary condiment for the crispy potatoes and has a wonderful way of managing to go with everything else on the plate.

1. Place the potatoes in a large pot, along with 2 tablespoons salt, and fill with enough water to cover by 1 inch. Bring to a boil over high heat, then reduce the heat to a simmer and cook, uncovered, until the potatoes are *just* tender when pierced with a fork, 10 to 15 minutes. (Be careful not to overcook!) Transfer to a colander to drain, then return to the pot off the heat for a minute or two to help any remaining moisture evaporate.

2. Meanwhile, preheat the oven to 450°F and brush a sheet pan all over with 1 tablespoon of the olive oil.

3. Arrange the potatoes on the prepared sheet pan. Using the bottom of a measuring cup or drinking glass, gently smash each one until it's about ½ inch thick. Drizzle the potatoes with 3 tablespoons of the olive oil and carefully flip to coat both sides in oil. Sprinkle with ½ teaspoon salt and a few grinds of black pepper. Roast the potatoes until golden brown and crisp at the edges, 30 to 40 minutes.

4. **While the potatoes roast, make the salsa verde:** In a small bowl, combine the parsley, mint, capers, scallion, garlic, vinegar, the remaining 2 tablespoons olive oil, and ¼ teaspoon salt. Whisk together and set aside.

5. Transfer the roasted potatoes to a serving platter. Spoon the salsa verde over the potatoes, including any liquid left in the bowl. Sprinkle the potatoes lightly with salt and pepper, and serve hot.

GET AHEAD
You can boil the potatoes, let them cool completely, then refrigerate them in a sealed container for up to 3 days before resuming the recipe at step 2.

Coconut Creamed Corn

⅓ cup unsweetened coconut flakes

1 (13.5-ounce) can unsweetened full-fat coconut milk

4 cups fresh corn kernels (about 5 to 7 ears of corn; see Tip)

1 teaspoon kosher salt, plus more to taste

2 teaspoons freshly squeezed lime juice

⅓ cup thinly sliced chives or scallions (about 2 scallions)

¼ teaspoon chipotle chile powder

In the two months when corn is in season in New York, I find ways to use it in almost everything I cook. Just ask my husband, who jokes that I have a secret contract with "Big Corn."

This coconut creamed corn is a simple summer side I like to serve with grilled steak. Made with coconut milk, lime juice, toasted coconut flakes, and a pinch of chipotle powder, it's creamy and rich—without any actual cream—and full of bright, fresh flavors. The corn is cooked until tender but not falling apart, making for lots of nice crunch in each bite.

1. In a 12-inch skillet, toast the coconut flakes over medium heat, tossing often, until golden brown, 3 to 5 minutes. Transfer to a small bowl and set aside. Let the skillet cool completely, then wipe it out with a paper towel.

2. Pour the coconut milk into the same skillet and whisk gently until smooth. Add the corn kernels and salt and bring to a boil over medium-high heat. Reduce the heat and simmer, stirring occasionally, until the coconut milk has reduced, 20 to 25 minutes—it should no longer pool at the sides of the pan when you pull the edges of the corn in toward the center of the pan with a wooden spoon.

3. Off the heat, stir in the lime juice, half the scallions, and the chipotle powder. Taste and season with salt if necessary. Garnish with the toasted coconut flakes and remaining scallions and serve immediately.

TIP

To remove corn kernels from the cob, slice off the end of the cob to create a flat surface, and stand the cob up on the cut end in a large bowl. Carefully cut down the sides of the cob to remove the kernels.

Brussels Sprouts
with Dates & Crispy Prosciutto

SERVES 4 TO 6

1 ounce thinly sliced
prosciutto

1½ pounds Brussels sprouts,
trimmed and halved (or
quartered if large)

3 tablespoons extra-virgin
olive oil

½ teaspoon kosher salt

⅓ cup chopped pitted dates

1 tablespoon balsamic vinegar

Crispy prosciutto is one of my favorite little back-pocket cooking tricks: it adds instant salt and a sort of savory sweetness to any roasted vegetable, pasta, or even avocado toast. I love it on these simply roasted Brussels sprouts, along with chopped dates and a drizzle of balsamic vinegar. This recipe would make a fun twist on holiday Brussels sprouts, or a delicious accompaniment to any wintry main course.

1. Preheat the oven to 400°F.

2. Spread the prosciutto slices on a sheet pan and bake until crisp, about 10 minutes. Transfer the prosciutto to a plate and set aside to cool, reserving the sheet pan.

3. Place the Brussels sprouts on the pan and drizzle with the olive oil. Sprinkle with the salt and toss well. Arrange the Brussels sprouts so they're cut-sides down. Roast until the sprouts are tender and golden brown, 25 to 30 minutes, tossing halfway through.

4. Immediately add the dates and vinegar to the pan and toss well. Break the prosciutto into small pieces and scatter them over the Brussels sprouts.

5. Transfer everything to a serving platter and serve warm or at room temperature.

COOKING FOR A CROWD
Like the other roasted vegetables in this chapter, these sprouts need their space! If you're doubling the recipe, use 2 sheet pans or roast in batches.

Desserts

Peanut Butter & Ginger Cookies (PB&Gs)

1 stick (4 ounces/113 grams) unsalted butter, at room temperature

½ cup (125 grams) creamy all-natural peanut butter

½ cup (100 grams) granulated sugar

½ cup (100 grams) lightly packed light brown sugar

2 tablespoons (40 grams) molasses

1 large egg, at room temperature

1 cup (130 grams) all-purpose flour

½ teaspoon ground ginger

½ teaspoon kosher salt

¼ teaspoon baking powder

¼ teaspoon baking soda

⅓ cup (47 grams) finely chopped crystallized ginger

Recipe inspiration can strike anywhere, and this idea came to me as I was eating a piece of one of one my favorite candies, Chimes Ginger Chews. Chimes' founder, Elvis Sae-Tang, was inspired by the ginger candies from his parents' Javanese village and wanted to share the health benefits of these delicious treats with the world. Chimes makes several flavors, but peanut butter–ginger is my favorite: I love how the addition of peanut butter softens the candy's gingery kick ever so slightly. I decided to play around with adding some ginger to my favorite peanut butter cookies and stumbled upon something even more delicious than I'd imagined. A cross between peanut butter cookies and spiced molasses cookies, these are thin, crisp, and chewy, and it is very easy to eat very many of them.

1. In a stand mixer fitted with the paddle attachment (or in a large bowl using a hand mixer), combine the butter, peanut butter, granulated sugar, brown sugar, and molasses and mix on low speed until combined. Raise the speed to medium-high speed and mix until light and fluffy, about 3 minutes, scraping the sides and bottom of the bowl once or twice.

2. With the mixer on low, add the egg and mix until fully incorporated. Scrape down the sides and bottom of the bowl with a rubber spatula.

3. In a medium bowl, whisk together the flour, ground ginger, salt, baking powder, and baking soda.

4. With the mixer still on low, gradually add the dry ingredients and mix until just combined. Fold in the crystallized ginger and place the bowl of cookie dough in the refrigerator for at least 30 minutes and up to 1 hour.

5. When you're ready to bake, preheat the oven to 350°F and line two sheet pans with parchment paper.

6. Scoop two-tablespoon balls of dough onto the prepared sheet pan, spacing the cookies a couple of inches apart and dividing them evenly between the two pans.

7. Bake one pan at a time until the cookies are just starting to brown at the edges but are still soft to the touch, 14 to 16 minutes. The cookies should be slightly puffed, but they will flatten and firm up as they cool. Let cool for 10 minutes on the pan before carefully transferring to a wire rack to finish cooling.

8. These cookies are best eaten within 4 days. Store at room temperature in a sealed container.

Banana Cake with Dark Chocolate Frosting & Sea Salt

SERVES 12 TO 15

For the cake

Nonstick cooking spray, for the pan

2 cups mashed ripe bananas (about 4 large bananas)

1 cup (200 grams) granulated sugar

1 cup (200 grams) lightly packed light brown sugar

3 large eggs, at room temperature

¾ cup (155 grams) unrefined coconut oil, melted, or vegetable oil

1 cup (240 grams) sour cream, at room temperature

1 teaspoon vanilla extract

3 cups (390 grams) all-purpose flour

1½ teaspoons baking soda

1 teaspoon kosher salt

½ teaspoon ground cinnamon

For the frosting

9 ounces (255 grams) dark chocolate (70 to 85% cacao), broken into pieces (see Tip)

¼ cup (60 grams) heavy cream, at room temperature

1 teaspoon instant espresso powder

2 sticks (8 ounces/226 grams) unsalted butter, at room temperature

1 cup (110 grams) confectioners' sugar, sifted

Flaky sea salt, for serving

This cake is an ever so slightly elevated version of one of my childhood favorites: banana bread with chocolate chips. Made with ripe bananas and a hint of cinnamon and coconut, the cake is moist and balanced, but it's the generous layer of dark chocolate frosting and sprinkle of sea salt that really puts it over the top. What I love about sheet cakes is that they can feel either casual or festive, depending on when you serve them. This cake would make a spectacular grown-up birthday cake, studded with tall candles, or a delicious weekend treat for no reason at all.

1. Preheat the oven to 350°F. Grease a 9 × 13-inch cake pan with cooking spray and line the bottom with parchment paper.

2. In a large bowl, combine the banana, granulated sugar, brown sugar, eggs, coconut oil, sour cream, and vanilla and whisk until smooth and only small lumps remain. In a separate medium bowl, whisk together the flour, baking soda, salt, and cinnamon. Pour the dry ingredients into the wet ingredients and mix with a wooden spoon until combined. Don't overmix.

3. Pour the cake batter into the prepared pan, smoothing it into an even layer with a spatula. Bake until a cake tester inserted in the center comes out clean and the top of the cake springs back when lightly pressed, 35 to 40 minutes.

4. Let the cake cool for 30 minutes in the pan, then invert it onto a large board. Remove the parchment paper, then invert it back onto a serving platter and let cool completely. (You can also frost and serve the cake directly from the pan.)

5. **Meanwhile, make the frosting:** Place the chocolate in a heatproof bowl set over a pan of simmering water. Heat, stirring occasionally, until the chocolate has melted and is smooth. Set aside until completely cool.

6. While the chocolate cools, combine the heavy cream and espresso powder in a small glass measuring cup and whisk to dissolve the espresso powder.

7. In a stand mixer fitted with the paddle attachment, beat the butter on medium-high speed until fluffy and pale yellow, 2 to 3 minutes. On medium-low speed, add the confectioners' sugar and beat until smooth. With the mixer running, gradually add the heavy cream mixture and increase the speed to medium-high until incorporated, scraping down the bowl as necessary.

8. With the mixer on medium speed, gradually add the cooled chocolate. Mix, scraping the sides of the bowl as necessary, until combined and smooth.

9. Spread the frosting over the cooled cake. Sprinkle with sea salt, cut into squares, and serve at room temperature.

TIP

Use a good-quality dark chocolate with the percentage of cocoa solids somewhere between 70% and 85%. Bars of dark chocolate are often sold with other candy bars, not in the baking aisle.

GET AHEAD

This cake can be made in advance and stored at room temperature, wrapped well, for up to 24 hours before frosting and serving. Once frosted, the cake is best eaten the same day.

Strawberry Rhubarb Shortcake
with Buttermilk Biscuits

SERVES 8

Strawberry shortcake is a classic all-American dessert, but have you tried strawberry-*rhubarb* shortcake?! Hot pink slivers of tart, roasted rhubarb mixed in with the strawberries make for a balanced and undeniably gorgeous dessert. Make these to finish off a dinner, graduation, Mother's Day, Memorial Day—anything you're celebrating during rhubarb season that merits an extra-special finale.

For the biscuits

¾ cup (175 grams) buttermilk, shaken

1 large egg

½ teaspoon almond extract (optional)

2½ cups (325 grams) all-purpose flour, plus more for rolling

⅓ cup (67 grams) granulated sugar, plus more for sprinkling

1 tablespoon baking powder

1 teaspoon kosher salt

10 tablespoons (5 ounces/ 140 grams) cold unsalted butter, diced

1 large egg beaten with 1 tablespoon water, for the egg wash

For the fruit

1 pound rhubarb stalks, trimmed

⅓ cup freshly squeezed orange juice (1 orange)

2 to 3 tablespoons granulated sugar, as needed

1 pound strawberries, hulled and cut into slices ¼-inch thick

Lightly Sweetened Whipped Cream (page 203), for serving

1. **First, make the biscuits:** In a small bowl, whisk together the buttermilk, egg, and almond extract, if using.

2. In a large bowl, combine the flour, sugar, baking powder, and salt and whisk until well combined. Add the butter and, working quickly, work the butter into the flour using your hands or a pastry cutter, until it forms crumbles about the size of large peas. Switch to a fork and, stirring constantly, add the buttermilk mixture in a slow, steady steam. Mix just until a wet, sticky dough forms.

3. Dump the dough out onto a floured surface. Coat your hands in flour and working quickly pat the dough into a rectangle ¾-inch thick. Cut the dough into 4 pieces that are roughly equal in size, then stack them on top of each other and pat the dough back into a ¾-inch-thick rectangle, about 8 by 9 inches, tossing a bit more flour underneath if the dough is beginning to stick. Using a floured 2½-inch biscuit cutter, cut out 8 biscuits and place them on a lightly floured plate. If needed, gently reform any dough scraps into a ¾-inch-thick rectangle and cut out the remaining biscuits. Chill for at least 30 minutes before baking, or for up to 6 hours, covered in plastic wrap.

4. When ready to bake, preheat the oven to 400°F and line a sheet pan with parchment paper.

5. Place the biscuits, evenly spaced, on the pan. Brush with the egg wash, sprinkle lightly with sugar, and bake until just beginning to brown on top, about 18 minutes. Set the biscuits aside to cool completely and reduce the oven temperature to 350°F.

6. **Make the filling:** Cut any rhubarb stalks wider than 1-inch in half lengthwise and slice all the rhubarb crosswise on the diagonal into 1-inch pieces. Place in a baking dish just large enough to fit all the rhubarb in one layer. Add the orange juice and 2 tablespoons sugar and toss. If your rhubarb is pale pink or green in some places, add an additional tablespoon of sugar.

RECIPE CONTINUES

7. Bake until the rhubarb is fork tender but not falling apart, about 20 minutes. Cool for 15 minutes, then add the strawberries to the baking dish, toss, and set aside until completely cool.

8. To serve, break or slice the biscuits in half and place on dessert plates. Spoon a generous heap of fruit over the bottom half of the biscuit, along with some of the juices. Top with a large dollop of whipped cream and serve immediately.

GET AHEAD

Biscuits are always a little bit of an effort, but these don't require any special equipment, and you can make them earlier in the day so all you have to do is assemble the shortcakes before serving.

Dirty Blondies
with Chocolate, Hazelnut & Coffee

MAKES 9 BLONDIES

Softened butter and flour, for greasing the pan

¾ cup (105 grams) hazelnuts

1 stick (4 ounces/113 grams) unsalted butter, melted and slightly cooled

¾ cup (150 grams) lightly packed light brown sugar

1 large egg

1 large egg yolk

1 teaspoon vanilla extract

¼ teaspoon ground coffee

1 cup (130 grams) all-purpose flour

½ teaspoon baking powder

½ teaspoon kosher salt

1 (3-ounce/85-gram) bar good-quality milk chocolate, coarsely chopped

1 (3-ounce/85-gram) bar semisweet chocolate, coarsely chopped

Flaky sea salt, for sprinkling

If you ask me, blondies and brownies, like apples and oranges, should not be compared. They are distinctly different desserts, and blondies never benefit from the comparison. Brownies are a stand-alone treat, but a good blondie has a rich butterscotch flavor and chewy texture that makes it the ideal base for other add-ins—in this case, chunks of semisweet and milk chocolate, toasted hazelnuts, and a pinch of ground coffee. Add a generous sprinkle of flaky sea salt and these over-the-top delicious bars will have you asking, Brownie who?

Dirty Blondies are a decadent treat when cut into big squares, but I also like to slice them into 1-inch squares to serve after dinner or as part of a larger dessert spread.

1. Preheat the oven to 350°F. Butter an 8 × 8-inch baking pan, line the bottom with parchment paper, then butter and flour the pan.

2. Place the hazelnuts on a sheet pan and roast until the nuts are well-toasted and the skins have begun to split, about 10 minutes. Set aside until cool enough to handle, then roll the hazelnuts between your hands to remove the skins (it's fine if they don't all come off). Roughly chop the hazelnuts and set aside.

3. In a large bowl, combine the melted butter, brown sugar, whole egg, egg yolk, vanilla, and coffee and whisk until smooth.

4. In a small bowl, combine the flour, baking powder, and kosher salt. Gradually mix the dry ingredients into the wet ingredients and stir until just combined, making sure to scrape the bottom and sides of the bowl. Add both chocolates and the hazelnuts and mix until just combined.

5. Scrape the batter into the prepared pan, smooth the top with a spatula, and sprinkle with flaky sea salt. Bake until the edges of the blondies are golden brown and the center is just set, 23 to 25 minutes. (Don't overbake! See Tips.)

6. Cool completely in the pan before cutting the blondies into 9 bars (see Tips). Blondies are best eaten within 3 days. Store at room temperature or in the refrigerator in a sealed container.

TIPS

The key here is to slightly underbake the blondies, or they will turn out more cakey than fudgy.

For neater slicing, chill the cooled blondies in the fridge for at least 2 hours before cutting them into squares.

Perfect Little Chocolate Puddings

SERVES 8 TO 12

2 large egg yolks

½ cup (100 grams) granulated sugar

¼ cup (30 grams) cornstarch

¾ teaspoon kosher salt

½ cup (120 grams) heavy cream

3½ cups (840 grams) whole milk

8 ounces (227 grams) good-quality semisweet chocolate, chopped

1 teaspoon vanilla extract

½ teaspoon instant espresso powder

Lightly Sweetened Whipped Cream (page 203), for serving

The Mermaid Inn is a cozy seafood restaurant in New York known for their Monday oyster happy hour and the tiny chocolate puddings they send out with every check in lieu of a dessert menu. It's a simple and brilliant touch. The arrival of the little white ramekins on the table feels like a gift from the restaurant, and a tiny, post-dinner pot of rich chocolate hits exactly the right note every time.

At home, when you're making something particularly rich for dinner, it doesn't always feel right to go overboard with dessert—and yet, dinner feels incomplete without something sweet. So, taking a cue from the Mermaid Inn, I like to make these little chocolate puddings in individual dishes and bring them out at the opportune moment.

This recipe makes 8 generously sized portions, but you could easily stretch it to 12 or more if you serve it in small glasses or ramekins. I like to top the pudding with a spoonful of lightly whipped cream or, at Christmastime, a pinch of crushed candy cane.

1. Place the egg yolks in a medium bowl set near the stove. Place a fine-mesh sieve over a large bowl and set aside.

2. In a large heavy-bottomed saucepan, whisk together the sugar, cornstarch, and salt. Whisking gently, slowly pour in the heavy cream and whisk until smooth. Stir in the milk, set the pan over medium heat, and cook, stirring occasionally, until you start to see steam rising from the pan, about 8 minutes.

3. Reduce the heat to medium-low. Whisking the egg yolks constantly, use a measuring cup to pour about ⅓ cup of the hot milk mixture into the bowl with the egg yolks. Working quickly, repeat two or three more times, until the egg yolk mixture is warm to the touch. While stirring the milk in the saucepan, gradually pour the warmed egg mixture into the pan.

4. Cook, stirring often and scraping the bottom and sides of the pan, until the pudding comes to a simmer, about 3 minutes. (The consistency should seem slightly thin for pudding at this point; the pudding will thicken as it cools.)

5. Off the heat, stir in the chocolate, vanilla, and espresso powder. Stir until the chocolate has melted and the pudding is completely smooth.

6. Immediately pour the pudding through the sieve into the bowl beneath, scraping the underside of the sieve with a spatula. Press a piece of plastic wrap onto the surface of the pudding. This will prevent a skin from forming on top of the pudding.

7. Refrigerate for 3 hours, or until well chilled. To serve, spoon the pudding into serving dishes and top with whipped cream.

RECIPE CONTINUES ON PAGE 203

LIGHTLY SWEETENED WHIPPED CREAM

This is the simple, ever-so-slightly-sweet whipped cream
that I serve with most desserts.

Makes about 2 cups

1 cup cold heavy cream

1 tablespoon confectioners' sugar

In stand mixer fitted with the whisk attachment, beat the heavy cream and sugar
on medium speed until the cream begins to thicken. Increase the speed to high
and beat just until soft peaks form. Do not overbeat.

Peaches & Cream Pie

1⅓ cups (160 grams) graham cracker crumbs (from 10 or 11 cracker sheets)

¼ cup (50 grams) granulated sugar

¼ teaspoon ground cinnamon

¼ teaspoon kosher salt

6 tablespoons (3 ounces/ 85 grams) unsalted butter, melted

2 ounces (57 grams) cream cheese, at room temperature

½ cup (55 grams) confectioners' sugar, sifted

1 cup (240 grams) cold heavy cream

1 teaspoon vanilla extract

2 pounds yellow peaches (5 to 7 peaches)

Briermere Farms in Riverhead, New York, is a roadside farmstand famous for its fruit pies, made with their own stone fruit and berries. Of all their delicious pies and baked goods, my favorite is the fruit and cream pie, in which a mound of fresh fruit is piled high above a layer of whipped cream and a pastry crust.

This recipe is a riff on the Briermere pie, a version of which I originally shared with the *New York Times*. I swapped in a graham cracker crust in place of Briermere's pastry crust, which is easier to make and exactly what I want to eat with my fruit and whipped cream. I also add a little bit of cream cheese to the whipped cream, which gives it a slight tang and helps it hold up under the weight of the obscene amount of fruit on top.

When you cut into this pie, the mountain of fruit comes tumbling down—a delicious avalanche, but one that makes it hard to slice perfectly neat pieces. I say this for the perfectionists out there: This pie is supposed to be messy—it's part of the fun!

1. Preheat the oven to 350°F.

2. In a medium bowl, combine the graham cracker crumbs, granulated sugar, cinnamon, and salt. Add the melted butter and toss until the crumbs are moistened. Transfer the mixture to a 9-inch pie pan and press into an even layer on the bottom and sides of the pie pan, packing the crust lightly with the bottom of a measuring cup. Place the pie pan on a sheet pan and bake until set, 10 to 12 minutes. Cool completely.

3. In a stand mixer fitted with the paddle attachment (or in a large bowl with a hand mixer), combine the cream cheese and confectioners' sugar. Beat on low speed until combined, then increase the speed to high and beat until the mixture is smooth and creamy. Add the heavy cream and vanilla and beat on high speed until the mixture forms medium-stiff peaks.

4. Spread the whipped cream mixture onto the cooled crust, smooth the top, and refrigerate for at least 2 hours, or overnight, until set. (Cover with plastic wrap if chilling the pie overnight.)

5. Within an hour of serving, slice the peaches into ½-inch wedges. Spoon them onto the filling, covering the entire surface of the pie. Set aside until ready to serve, then cut into big wedges and dig in.

TIP

Crush the graham crackers in a food processor, or place them in a large Ziplock bag and crush them with a rolling pin.

SIMPLE SWAP

When peaches aren't in season, use blueberries or hulled strawberries.

GET AHEAD

While this pie needs to be finished just before serving to prevent the peaches from brownng, you can make the crust and spread on the whipped cream filling up to 24 hours in advance. Store, covered, in the refrigerator, until ready to serve.

Almost-Famous 4th of July Ice Cream Sandwiches

MAKES 8 GIANT ICE
CREAM SANDWICHES

16 Blueberry Muffin Sugar
Cookies (recipe follows)

2 (1-pint) containers
strawberry ice cream

For years, these ice cream sandwiches have lived in my metaphorical top-secret recipe vault, only coming out once a year when I make them for my family's 4th of July party. I've made other ice cream sandwiches, but these are the ones that are requested every year and rationed in the freezer until they run out.

Secret recipes are fun, but so much of the joy of creating recipes for me is knowing that other people can make and enjoy them. When I started writing this book, I knew it was time to share this one.

Made with strawberry ice cream and fluffy blueberry muffin sugar cookies, these ice cream sandwiches combine two nostalgic flavors in a surprising way. I think that's what makes them so special—they taste both familiar and brand-new at the same time.

If you've made ice cream sandwiches, you know they're a labor of love, but worth every minute for the reactions when you announce you've made homemade ice cream sandwiches. It's almost not even worth cooking dinner—if you're serving these, no one will remember anything else you made. I guess I should say, make these at your own risk, because you, too, may end up having to make them every 4th of July for the rest of your life.

1. Place the cookies in the refrigerator to firm up for at least 1 hour before assembling the ice cream sandwiches.

2. Allow the ice cream to soften slightly, about 10 minutes, before assembling. To assemble the cookies, line up 8 cookies, flat-sides up, on a large cutting board. Using an ice cream scoop, scoop about ½ cup of ice cream onto each cookie. Place the remaining cookies, flat-sides down, on top of each sandwich. Press gently but firmly, until the ice cream spreads to the edge of the cookies. Use a spatula to smooth the edges of the ice cream for a professional-looking finish.

3. Transfer the sandwiches to a platter and immediately place in the freezer. Freeze until firm, at least 6 hours. Serve, or wrap well with parchment paper and store for up to 1 week in the freezer.

COOKING FOR A CROWD

This recipe makes 8 large ice cream sandwiches. If you want to make more, slightly smaller sandwiches to feed a larger group, use the same cookie recipe but use 2 tablespoons dough for each cookie, and bake for about 16 minutes. You should end up with enough cookies for 12 to 14 sandwiches.

Blueberry Muffin Sugar Cookies

MAKES 16 TO 18 COOKIES

2½ cups (325 grams) all-purpose flour

¼ cup (30 grams) cornstarch

1½ teaspoons baking powder

1 teaspoon kosher salt

Pinch of ground cinnamon

2 sticks (8 ounces/226 grams) unsalted butter, at room temperature

2 ounces (57 grams) cream cheese, at room temperature

¾ cup (150 grams) granulated sugar, plus more for sprinkling

½ cup (100 grams) lightly packed light brown sugar

1 large egg, at room temperature

1½ teaspoons vanilla extract

1 cup (150 grams) blueberries, rinsed and patted dry

These cookies are an essential component of my ice cream sandwiches (see page 207), but they're a terrific cookie in their own right. Light and fluffy, with a hint of cinnamon and pockets of jammy blueberries, they're a perfect midmorning or afternoon snack with a cup of coffee. And, of course, if there were such a thing as a breakfast cookie, this would surely be it.

1. Preheat the oven to 350°F and line two sheet pans with parchment paper.

2. In a medium bowl, whisk together the flour, cornstarch, baking powder, salt, and cinnamon.

3. In a stand mixer fitted with the paddle attachment, beat the butter, cream cheese, granulated sugar, and brown sugar on medium-high speed until light and fluffy, about 3 minutes, scraping down the sides of the bowl as necessary. Add the egg and vanilla and mix until well combined. With the mixer on low, add the dry ingredients and mix until just combined. Use a spatula to gently fold in the blueberries by hand.

4. Scoop 3-tablespoon balls of dough onto the prepared pans, dividing them evenly between the pans and spacing them apart. Bake one pan at a time, until the cookies are just starting to brown at the edges but are still soft to the touch, 20 to 22 minutes.

5. Cool for 10 minutes on the pan, then transfer to a wire rack to cool completely. Store in a sealed container at room temperature for up to 3 days.

Candy's Flourless Chocolate Cake

SERVES 10 TO 12

Softened butter and
granulated sugar, for the pan

1 pound (454 grams)
semisweet chocolate (60% to
65% cacao), coarsely chopped

2 sticks (8 ounces/226 grams)
unsalted butter, cubed

7 large eggs, at room
temperature, separated

1 teaspoon vanilla extract

8 tablespoons (100 grams)
granulated sugar

⅛ teaspoon cream of tartar

¼ teaspoon kosher salt

Unsweetened cocoa powder,
for dusting

Unsweetened whipped cream
or crème fraîche, for serving

Grated orange zest, for
serving

My very appropriately named Aunt Candy is an incredibly talented pastry chef, who just so happened to marry another incredibly talented chef, my Uncle Mike. Family holidays at their house are the best.

Having grown up eating so many of Candy's desserts, I'm honored to include one of her signature recipes in this book. Her flourless chocolate cake has always been one of my favorites. It's intensely chocolatey and rich but also light and airy in texture. It's a pure chocolate delivery system, and cut into small slices, it can feed quite a crowd.

The caliber of the chocolate you use makes a big difference here, so make it with the best quality chocolate you can find. Candy makes it with Callebaut chocolate; Valrhona and Guittard are two other excellent brands that are widely available.

You can dress up this cake with fresh berries, or serve it simply, as I do, with a spoonful of whipped cream and a sprinkle of orange zest.

1. Preheat the oven to 425°F and arrange a rack in the center of the oven. Butter a 9-inch springform pan and line the bottom with parchment paper. Sprinkle the sides of the pan with sugar, tapping the pan to remove any excess, and place on a sheet pan to catch any drips.

2. In a large heatproof bowl, combine the chocolate and butter and set over a pan of simmering water. Cook, stirring occasionally, until melted and smooth. Set aside off the heat, stirring occasionally, until the mixture is cool to the touch.

3. Meanwhile, in a medium bowl, combine the egg yolks, vanilla, and 2 tablespoons of the sugar. Whisk vigorously until the sugar has dissolved and the mixture has lightened in color, about 2 minutes. (It takes longer than you think!) Add the egg mixture to the cooled chocolate and whisk until smooth and glossy.

4. In a stand mixer fitted with the whisk attachment, combine the egg whites, cream of tartar, and salt and whisk on high speed until frothy. With the mixer running, gradually add the remaining 6 tablespoons sugar, 1 tablespoon at a time, waiting a few seconds after each addition. Whip until the meringue forms semi-firm peaks.

5. Add a few spoonfuls of the meringue to the chocolate mixture and fold them in with a rubber spatula. Continue adding spoonfuls of meringue, folding gently to avoid deflating the meringue, until all of it has been added and the batter is uniform in color.

6. Immediately pour the batter into the prepared pan and gently smooth the top. Bake until the edges are set but the center of the cake still has a slight wobble, 16 to 18 minutes.

RECIPE CONTINUES

7. Cool the cake completely in the pan, then refrigerate for at least 2 hours to set.

8. Run a paring knife around the edges of the cake, then release the pan sides and carefully invert the cake onto a board. Remove the bottom of the springform pan, then place the cake, right-side up, on a serving platter. Dust the top with cocoa powder and serve in narrow wedges, chilled or at room temperature, with unsweetened whipped cream and a sprinkle of orange zest. This cake keeps for up to 5 days, well-wrapped, in the refrigerator.

GET AHEAD
While it might be tempting to cut into this cake while it's still warm, it's crucial to let it cool completely and set in the refrigerator for the perfect, super-smooth, and creamy texture (and for easy slicing). The upside is all that chilling makes this cake an ideal one to make in advance!

Rainbow Sprinkle Ice Cream Cake

SERVES 12

24 Oreo cookies (10 ounces)

½ teaspoon kosher salt

6 tablespoons (3 ounces/ 85 grams) unsalted butter, melted and slightly cooled

3 (14-ounce) containers cookies & cream or chocolate ice cream

2 ounces (57 grams) cream cheese

½ cup (55 grams) confectioners' sugar

1 cup (240 grams) cold heavy cream

½ teaspoon vanilla extract

½ cup rainbow sprinkles

Hot fudge (optional), for serving

Living in the Hamptons may sound like a dream, and it was in many respects, but one challenge of spending my twenties in a largely vacation/weekend community was that people my age didn't often live there for long. They'd come for a year to try living at the beach, or move to the Hamptons when their jobs brought them there for the summer season. It was fun in a way, always making new friends, but it was also hard to watch people I'd gotten to know pack up and leave.

Through a stroke of kismet, my old high school friend Paul Weinstein also ended up living in East Hampton after college. Over the years, we celebrated birthdays, promotions, and relationships and cooked more dinners together than I can count.

At some point, Paul's mom sent me her ice cream cake recipe to make for his birthday, and it became an unofficial annual tradition.

You can use whatever flavor of ice cream you like, but be sure to use a premium ice cream brand—like Häagen-Dazs—if possible. The pricier brands have less air in them—and more ice cream—and the richer the ice cream, the firmer the cake will be, and you'll get much neater slices.

1.   Line a 9 × 9-inch baking pan with two crisscrossed sheets of parchment, leaving 2 inches of overhang on all four sides.

2.   In a food processor, combine the Oreos and salt and process until the cookies are very finely ground. Add the melted butter and pulse until the crumbs are moistened. Transfer the crumb mixture to the prepared pan and press into an even layer. Place the pan in the freezer until the crust is firm to the touch, 30 to 45 minutes.

3.   Meanwhile, when the crust has about 15 minutes to go, soften the ice cream at room temperature for 10 to 15 minutes, until easy to scoop but not melted.

4.   Scoop large spoonfuls of ice cream all over the chilled crust and work quickly with an offset spatula or wooden spoon to smooth the ice cream into an even layer with no gaps. Place the cake in the freezer for at least 1 hour, until the ice cream is firm to the touch.

5.   In a stand mixer fitted with the paddle attachment or in a large bowl with a hand mixer), beat the cream cheese and confectioners' sugar on low speed until combined. Increase the speed to high and whip until the mixture is smooth and creamy. Add the heavy cream and vanilla and beat on high speed until the mixture forms soft peaks.

RECIPE CONTINUES

6. Spread the whipped cream over the cake and smooth into an even layer. Sprinkle the rainbow sprinkles on top, cover the pan with plastic wrap, and freeze until firm, at least 4 hours or overnight.

7. To serve, lift the overhanging parchment paper to remove the cake. Discard the parchment paper and place the cake on a rimmed platter. Cut into pieces and serve immediately, drizzled with hot fudge, if using.

GET AHEAD

Frozen desserts are ideal for making in advance because, in fact, you *have* to make them in advance! This cake keeps well for up to a week in the freezer. Just be sure to wrap it very tightly with plastic wrap so no air gets in—that's what causes freezer burn!

Roasted Pears with Brandy & Brown Sugar

4 firm-ripe Bartlett or Bosc pears

¼ cup (50 grams) lightly packed light brown sugar

½ teaspoon kosher salt, plus more for serving

4 tablespoons Cognac or other brandy, divided

4 tablespoons (2 ounces/ 57 grams) unsalted butter, diced

Crème fraîche or unsweetened whipped cream, for serving

Looking for an elegant-but-easy dinner party dessert? How about one with very few ingredients and very few dishes involved? I have just the one. In this French bistro–inspired dessert, pears are sprinkled with butter, brown sugar, and a splash of brandy and roasted until beautifully caramelized and tender. The flavors in this recipe are deceptively simple: as the pears roast, their juices mix with the brandy and brown sugar, forming the most delicious, toffee-like pan sauce. I like to serve these with a spoonful of crème fraîche or whipped cream, a drizzle of sauce from the pan—and little glasses of dessert wine if I'm feeling fancy.

1. Preheat the oven to 375°F.

2. Cut the pears in half through the stem and remove the core using a melon baller or small spoon. Place the pears, cut-sides up, in a baking dish just large enough to hold them in one layer. Sprinkle them with the brown sugar and salt, then pour 2 tablespoons of the brandy over them.

3. Flip the pears so they are cut-sides down. Scatter the diced butter over them and bake, uncovered, until fork-tender and lightly caramelized, 30 to 40 minutes, depending on how ripe they are.

4. Flip the pears so they are cut-sides up and spoon the pan sauce over them. Pour the remaining 2 tablespoons brandy over the pears and bake for 5 minutes to thicken the sauce.

5. Transfer the pears to individual dessert plates, placing 2 halves on each plate, drizzle with any remaining sauce, and serve with crème fraîche or a spoonful of unsweetened whipped cream.

Skillet Apple Crisp
with Shortbread Crumble

SERVES 6 TO 8

For the shortbread crumble

1½ sticks (6 ounces/
170 grams) unsalted butter,
at room temperature

½ cup (100 grams) lightly
packed light brown sugar

1½ cups (195 grams) all-
purpose flour

¼ teaspoon kosher salt

¼ cup (28 grams) old-
fashioned rolled oats

For the apple filling

3 tablespoons unsalted butter

¼ cup (50 grams) lightly
packed light brown sugar

1½ teaspoons ground
cinnamon

½ teaspoon ground ginger

¼ teaspoon ground nutmeg

Pinch of ground cloves

¼ teaspoon kosher salt

1½ pounds Granny Smith
apples (about 3 large), peeled
and ¾-inch diced

1½ pounds Honeycrisp apples
(about 3 medium), peeled,
cored and ¾-inch diced

3 tablespoons freshly
squeezed lemon juice
(1 large lemon)

2 teaspoons cornstarch

Vanilla ice cream, for serving

If you like to bake, you've probably made apple crisp. Most recipes go something like this: Toss chopped apples with sugar, lemon juice, and a bit of flour or cornstarch. Sprinkle a crumble topping on top and pop the whole thing in the oven until nice and browned. Sometimes this all works out great, but more often, the crumble is browned long before the apples are tender and the juices have had a chance to reduce and thicken into a delicious sauce.

My trick for perfect apple crisp every time is to precook the apple mixture in a skillet. That way, the apples have plenty of time to get soft and gooey and the sauce is already nice and thick when the crisp goes into the oven. When the crumble topping is browned, you can take the dish out of the oven, confident that the apples underneath will be baked to perfection.

I make my topping with a simple shortbread dough, crumbled into pieces so it bakes into little chunks of golden shortbread cookie. If you want a more traditional apple crisp, swap in the streusel topping from Maine Pumpkin Buckle (page 236).

1. Preheat the oven to 350°F.

2. **First, make the shortbread crumble:** In a stand mixer fitted with the paddle attachment, combine the butter and brown sugar and mix on medium speed just until smooth. Add the flour and salt and mix on low speed until the dough starts to come together, scraping the side and bottom of the bowl as necessary. Add the oats and mix until combined and small clumps begin to form. Place the bowl in the refrigerator while you make the apple filling.

3. **Make the apple filling:** In a 10-inch cast-iron skillet, combine the butter, brown sugar, cinnamon, ginger, nutmeg, cloves, and salt and cook over medium heat until the butter has melted. Add half the apples, along with the lemon juice, and cook, tossing often, until the apples are beginning to soften and release their juices, 4 to 6 minutes. Add the rest of the apples and cook until the second batch of apples have started to soften, 4 to 6 minutes longer.

4. Spoon a few tablespoons of liquid from the skillet into a small bowl. Add the cornstarch and whisk until smooth, then return the mixture to the skillet, using a small spatula to scrape the bowl. Cook until the liquid in the pan starts to thicken, about 1 more minute, then remove the pan from the heat.

5. Crumble the chilled shortbread dough into pieces and sprinkle them all over the surface of the apples. Place the skillet on a sheet pan and bake until the fruit is bubbling and the crumbs are nicely browned, 30 to 40 minutes. Cool for 15 minutes before serving alongside a scoop of vanilla ice cream.

GET AHEAD

You can make the apple filling, allow it to cool completely, then top it with the shortbread crumble. Place, covered, in the fridge for up to 8 hours before baking and serving.

COOKING FOR A CROWD

If you find yourself in a need of giant apple crisp, you can double this recipe to serve 12 to 16. Cook the apples in two batches, then transfer them to a 9 x 13-inch baking dish, top with the shortbread crumble, and bake.

Lemon, Rosemary & Olive Oil Cake

SERVES 8 TO 10

1 cup (230 grams) extra-virgin olive oil

2 (4-inch) fresh rosemary sprigs

Nonstick cooking spray (with flour) for the pan

1½ cups (300 grams) granulated sugar

2 large eggs

½ teaspoon vanilla extract

⅔ cup (160 grams) sour cream

Grated zest of 2 lemons

⅓ cup (80 grams) freshly squeezed lemon juice (2 lemons)

2 cups (260 grams) all-purpose flour, plus more for greasing the pan

½ teaspoon baking powder

½ teaspoon baking soda

1 teaspoon kosher salt

Lightly Sweetened Whipped Cream (page 203) or confectioners' sugar, for serving

3 small oranges, for serving (optional; see Tip)

A few years ago I came up with a rosemary-infused olive oil for a savory recipe I was working on. I liked it so much that I started playing around with other ways to use it, and that led me here. If herbs and olive oil in a cake sounds odd, just trust me on this one. The cake is plenty sweet and very lemony, with just a hint of rosemary shining through.

If I'm making this for a special occasion, I dress it up with a pile of segmented oranges on top. But for an everyday treat, I skip the citrus and let the cake sit on the counter, watching it disappear—sliver by sliver—until there's nothing left. How you serve it is up to you!

1. In a small skillet or saucepan, combine the oil and rosemary sprigs. Bring to a simmer over medium heat until the rosemary begins to sizzle, then turn the heat to its lowest setting and cook for 5 minutes. Set aside to cool for 20 minutes, then discard the rosemary sprigs and pour the oil into a large bowl.

2. Meanwhile, position a rack in the center of the oven and preheat the oven to 350°F. Spray a 9-inch round cake pan at least 2 inches deep with cooking spray (see Tips), line the bottom with parchment paper, then flour the sides.

3. Add the sugar to the bowl with the rosemary oil and whisk until combined. Add the eggs and whisk vigorously until thick and glossy. Add the vanilla, sour cream, lemon zest, and lemon juice and whisk until smooth.

4. In a medium bowl, whisk together the flour, baking powder, baking soda, and salt. Pour the dry ingredients into the wet ingredients and whisk gently until only small lumps remain. Pour the batter into the prepared pan.

5. Bake until the edges of the cake are golden brown and a toothpick comes out clean, 55 minutes to 1 hour. Let cool for 30 minutes in the pan before inverting onto a wire rack to cool completely.

6. Serve the cake at room temperature, with Lightly Sweetened Whipped Cream or a sprinkle of confectioners' sugar and the orange segments, if using. Store covered at room temperature for up to 3 days.

TIPS

It's important that your cake pan be at least 2 inches deep. This is a tall cake and will overflow in shallow cake pans. A springform pan works, too.

To segment oranges, peel the oranges with a small, sharp knife, removing all the white pith. Cut carefully between the membranes to remove the orange sections.

Chewy Chocolate Cherry Cookies

MAKES 12 COOKIES

Nonstick cooking spray, for the pan

3 large egg whites, at room temperature

1 teaspoon vanilla extract

2½ cups (275 grams) confectioners' sugar, sifted

¾ cup (72 grams) unsweetened cocoa powder, sifted

½ teaspoon kosher salt

¼ teaspoon espresso powder (optional)

⅓ cup (50 grams) dried cherries

¼ cup (44 grams) dark chocolate chips (dairy-free if preferred)

This recipe is my little homage to the Mitten State. I spent summers as a kid with my family in the Upper Peninsula of Michigan, and it's the site of so many memories. It's where I learned to swim, to fish, and where I first learned to bake with my friends and cousins. With no TV in our cabin, rainy days were for playing board games, reading Harry Potter, and baking the occasional box of brownie mix.

These crinkly chocolate cookies start out with a meringue-like batter, but come out fudgy, rich, and chewy, not altogether dissimilar to a boxed brownie. And they're studded with tart, dried cherries—which happen to be Michigan's state fruit! We would have been much more likely to add mini marshmallows to our brownies than dried fruit back then, but I still like to think I would have enjoyed these as a kid.

1. Preheat the oven to 350°F and arrange the racks so they are evenly spaced in the oven. Line two sheet pans with parchment paper and spray the parchment lightly with cooking spray.

2. Place the egg whites and vanilla in a large bowl and whisk until lightly frothy, about 15 seconds. Add the confectioners' sugar, cocoa powder, salt, and espresso powder, if using, and whisk until incorporated. This will take a few minutes and the batter will be very thick, almost like frosting. With a wooden spoon, fold in the cherries and chocolate chips.

3. Spoon 6 (2-tablespoon) mounds of batter onto each prepared sheet pan, evenly spacing them, to form 12 cookies.

4. Bake the cookies until crackled on top and just set at the edges, 11 to 13 minutes. (The cookies will firm up as they cool.) Cool completely on the pans before transferring to a plate. Store cookies in a sealed container at room temperature for up to 3 days.

SIMPLE SWAP
You'd never know it from their rich flavor and fudgy texture, but these cookies are totally gluten-free. They can also be made dairy-free if you use dairy-free chocolate chips, such as Enjoy Life brand.

Breakfast
& Brunch

Overnight Oats
with Almond Butter & Strawberry Jam

SERVES 4

1 pound strawberries, hulled and chopped

2 tablespoons granulated sugar

2 teaspoons freshly squeezed lemon juice

2 cups old-fashioned rolled oats

4 tablespoons almond butter

2 cups milk (whole, low-fat, oat, or almond)

4 teaspoons maple syrup, divided

1 teaspoon vanilla extract, divided

Ground cinnamon

Kosher salt

I've waited until the end of this book to tell you that of all the exciting foods in this world, few make me happier than a simple bowl of oatmeal. I eat oatmeal in some form almost every morning. I eat it when traveling, when I'm not feeling well, with a million toppings, or just plain with a splash of milk. It's my ultimate comfort food.

When it's too warm for a bowl of hot oatmeal, I make overnight oats. (I know how to *live*!) A cousin to Swiss muesli, these are made by simply soaking the oats in milk overnight, until thick and creamy. They're a great canvas for different flavors and mix-ins, and my personal favorite combination is a scoop of almond butter, a splash of maple syrup, and a swirl of jam. And while I eat these most often as a quick weekday breakfast, mini jars of overnight oats would make a nice addition to a brunch spread.

1. In a large saucepan, combine the strawberries and sugar. Cook over medium heat, stirring often, until the berries release their juices and the liquid in the pan begins to thicken, 12 to 14 minutes. Off the heat, stir in the lemon juice. Transfer the jam to a medium bowl, cool completely, then refrigerate for at least 30 minutes or up to 24 hours.

2. Meanwhile, add ½ cup oats to each of four glass tumblers or 12-ounce jars. To each glass, add ½ cup milk, 1 tablespoon almond butter, 1 teaspoon maple syrup, ¼ teaspoon vanilla extract, a pinch of cinnamon, and a pinch of salt. Stir until well combined.

3. Cover and refrigerate for at least 3 hours or overnight, until thick. Spoon about ¼ cup of the jam into each glass and serve, or store in the fridge, covered, for up to 3 days.

SIMPLE SWAP

This quick homemade strawberry jam is an absolute delight, and not much work at all, but when time is of the essence, a scoop of your favorite jarred jam will do just fine.

COOKING FOR A CROWD

You could get 8 servings out of this recipe if you make half-size portions, using small (8-ounce) jars or glasses.

Everyday Granola

2 cups old-fashioned rolled oats

1 cup raw almonds, chopped

1 cup walnuts, chopped

½ teaspoon ground cinnamon

1 teaspoon kosher salt

⅓ cup canola or other neutral oil

¼ cup honey

Consider this recipe a basic canvas for homemade granola and feel free to make it your own. Mix up the nuts, and add some pumpkin seeds, sesame seeds, or coconut flakes. Experiment with different spices, or add a handful of dried fruit when the granola comes out of the oven. Or keep it simple and make it as written for a delicious breakfast or snack to eat all week long.

1. Preheat the oven to 275°F and line a sheet pan with parchment paper.

2. In a large bowl, combine the oats, almonds, walnuts, cinnamon, and salt. Add the oil and toss well. Add the honey and toss again. Transfer the granola mixture to the prepared pan and press into an even layer.

3. Bake until the oats are golden brown, 45 to 50 minutes, tossing twice throughout.

4. Press the granola lightly with the back of a wooden spoon and cool completely in the pan. Break the granola into clusters and store at room temperature for up to 1 week.

English Muffin Breakfast Bake

SERVES 8 TO 10

6 standard-size English muffins (from a 13-ounce package)

12 ounces good-quality lean bacon, cut crosswise into ¾-inch pieces

1 tablespoon maple syrup

12 large eggs

2½ cups whole milk

1½ teaspoons kosher salt

½ teaspoon freshly ground black pepper

1 tablespoon unsalted butter, for the baking dish

¼ cup minced fresh chives or scallions

8 ounces grated sharp cheddar cheese (2 cups)

My grandfather used to make a simple egg casserole with white bread soaked in milk, bacon, and Swiss cheese. His original recipe is still a family favorite and inspired me to come up with my own version when I first began writing recipes. Mine is inspired by the classic bacon, egg, and cheese breakfast sandwich, and I can promise, whether you're hosting weekend brunch, making breakfast on Christmas morning, or just trying to use up some on-their-way-out English muffins, it will be a huge crowd-pleaser. It's a "cook-pleaser," too, because you can assemble the whole thing the night before and bake it off in the morning. This recipe is so consistently popular on my site— and such a staple at my own house—that I had to include it here.

1. Preheat the oven to 350°F.

2. Cut the English muffins into 1-inch cubes. (Do not halve them horizontally as you would normally for the toaster.) Spread the cubes on a sheet pan and bake until lightly toasted, about 15 minutes.

3. Line a plate with paper towels. Place the bacon in a 12-inch skillet set over medium-high heat. Cook, tossing often, until crisp, 8 to 10 minutes. Using a slotted spoon, transfer to the paper towels and drizzle with the maple syrup.

4. In a large bowl, whisk together the eggs, milk, salt, and pepper.

5. To assemble, grease the bottom and sides of a 9 × 13-inch baking dish with the butter. Sprinkle half the bacon, half the chives, and half the cheese into the baking dish. Add the English muffin cubes on top in one even layer. Carefully pour the egg mixture into the pan, pressing down lightly to make sure all the muffin cubes are moistened. Top with the remaining bacon, cheese, and chives. Wrap well and refrigerate for at least 2 hours, or overnight.

6. Preheat the oven again to 350°F. Let the assembled dish sit at room temperature while the oven heats.

7. Bake until puffed and cooked through and the cheese is golden brown, 45 to 50 minutes. Cool for 10 minutes before cutting into squares and serving.

Winter Fruit Salad

SERVES 6

2 pounds oranges, such as Cara Cara, navel, blood oranges, or a mix

1 large ruby red grapefruit

1 ripe d'Anjou or other pear

Pinch of granulated sugar

Pinch of kosher salt

¼ cup pomegranate arils

2 teaspoons extra-virgin olive oil

3 tablespoons torn fresh mint leaves

Flaky sea salt, for serving (optional)

A good fruit salad is a must-have for any brunch spread. It may sound odd, but I like to dress my fruit salads the way I would a regular salad, with a sprinkle of salt and a drizzle of olive oil. Of course, fresh fruit is delicious on its own, but these savory additions add a richness that makes any bowl of fruit— but especially one with winter citrus—taste more like a composed dish than a fruit cup. In this recipe, I suggest using a mix of citrus so the salad is colorful, but please don't feel like you have to buy every kind of orange at the store. Two varieties will do just fine.

1. Using a small serrated knife, peel the oranges and grapefruit and trim to remove any remaining pith. Slice all the peeled fruit crosswise into thin rounds (no thicker than ½ inch), remove any visible seeds and pith, and place in a large bowl. Halve and core the pear, then cut crosswise into ¼-inch-thick slices and add to the bowl.

2. Add the sugar and kosher salt and toss gently. Arrange the fruit on a flat serving platter along with any juice that has accumulated in the bowl. Sprinkle the pomegranate arils on top, drizzle with the olive oil, and garnish with the mint and a sprinkle of flaky salt, if using, and serve.

GET AHEAD
The citrus fruits will continue to release their juices as the salad sits, so it is best served within 30 minutes of being dressed. To make in advance, cut and store the oranges and grapefruit, but don't dress them until ready to serve.

Maine Pumpkin Buckle

For the cake

Softened unsalted butter, for the pan

1 cup (235 grams) canned pumpkin puree

1 cup (200 grams) granulated sugar

2 large eggs

1 stick (4 ounces/113 grams) unsalted butter, melted and slightly cooled

¼ cup (60 grams) whole milk

2 tablespoons maple syrup

1 teaspoon vanilla extract

1¾ cups (228 grams) all-purpose flour

1 teaspoon kosher salt

1 teaspoon baking powder

½ teaspoon baking soda

1 teaspoon ground cinnamon

½ teaspoon ground ginger

½ teaspoon ground nutmeg

¼ teaspoon ground cloves

My alma mater, Bowdoin College, is known for having excellent dining hall food. I don't think my friends and I realized how good we had it at the time, and on cold mornings I still daydream about walking into that dining hall first thing in the morning, knowing there would be hot coffee, all my breakfast foods, and baked goods galore waiting for me.

Two of my favorite treats in regular rotation were the pumpkin buckle, a spiced pumpkin cake with a crumbly topping, and the pumpkin muffins with a cream cheese swirl running through the middle. I've combined them here into the pumpkin cake of my dreams.

I had a hard time deciding whether this recipe should be in the dessert or breakfast section. The cream cheese swirl and streusel topping definitely push it into dessert territory, but I still think of it as a breakfast cake at heart.

1. Preheat the oven to 350°F. Grease a 9-inch square baking pan with cooking spray or butter and line the bottom with parchment paper.

2. **Make the streusel:** In a medium bowl, combine the flour, brown sugar, butter, cinnamon, and salt and work with a fork or fingers until crumbly. Set side.

3. **Make the cream cheese swirl:** Place the cream cheese in a medium bowl and mix with a wooden spoon until smooth and creamy. Add the granulated sugar, egg, and vanilla and whisk until smooth. Set aside.

4. **Make the cake:** In a large bowl, combine the pumpkin, sugar, eggs, butter, milk, maple syrup, and vanilla and whisk until smooth. In a small bowl, whisk together the flour, salt, baking powder, baking soda, cinnamon, ginger, nutmeg, and cloves. Pour the dry ingredients into the wet ingredients and mix until just combined. (The batter will be slightly lumpy. Do not overmix.)

5. Pour about half the cake batter into the prepared pan, smoothing it into an even layer with a spatula. Dollop the cream cheese mixture onto the batter in large spoonfuls, and gently spread into an even layer. (It's okay if the layers begin to mix a little bit!) Add the rest of the cake batter in a large spoonfuls, spreading it out to cover the cream cheese.

For the streusel

½ cup (65 grams) all-purpose flour

½ cup (100 grams) lightly packed light brown sugar

4 tablespoons (2 ounces/ 57 grams) unsalted butter, at room temperature

¼ teaspoon ground cinnamon

Pinch of kosher salt

For the cream cheese swirl

8 ounces (226 grams) cream cheese, at room temperature

¼ cup (50 grams) granulated sugar

1 large egg, at room temperature

½ teaspoon vanilla extract

6. Run a butter knife through the batter in a swirl pattern, working your way around the pan until the cake and cream cheese are nicely swirled. Sprinkle the streusel over the cake.

7. Bake until puffed, set in the middle, and nicely browned on top, 40 to 50 minutes.

8. Let cool for at least 15 minutes in the pan before carefully transferring it to a serving platter. Or, cut into squares and serve directly from the pan. Serve warm or at room temperature.

Maine Pumpkin Buckle, page 236

Sweet Potato & Poblano Hash with Eggs

SERVES 2 TO 4

4 tablespoons extra-virgin olive oil, divided

1¼ pounds sweet potatoes, peeled and ½-inch diced (about 2 medium potatoes)

1½ cups (½-inch) diced poblano pepper (about 2 medium peppers)

1½ cups chopped yellow onion (1 medium onion)

¼ teaspoon chipotle chile powder

¼ teaspoon ground cumin

1 teaspoon kosher salt, plus more to taste

Freshly ground black pepper

1 medium garlic clove, minced

¼ cup thinly sliced scallions, divided (1 to 2 scallions)

2 teaspoons white wine vinegar

4 large eggs

¼ cup crumbled Cotija or plain goat cheese

Sliced avocado and toast, for serving

Hot sauce, for serving (optional)

A one-skillet hash and eggs is my go-to when I want to make a special breakfast at home but don't feel like doing a sink full of dishes first thing in the morning. (Of course, I never really feel like doing a sink full of dishes, but especially not before the day even gets rolling.) This particular hash is made with sweet potatoes, mild poblano peppers, and lots of onion and garlic. Chipotle chile powder and ground cumin give it a touch of smoky spice, but if you like a little more heat, add a dash of your favorite hot sauce. Finished with a sprinkle of scallions and Cotija cheese, it's a breakfast dish worthy of your favorite diner or brunch spot, made in the comfort of your own pajamas.

This recipe doesn't feed a crowd like my Red Potato & Leek Frittata with Goat Cheese & Dill (page 245) or English Muffin Breakfast Bake (page 232), but it will make a few good friends very happy, especially if there's an old *House Hunters* episode on TV, a big pot of coffee, and plenty of toast and sliced avocado on the side.

1. Preheat the oven to 375°F.

2. Heat a 12-inch ovenproof skillet over medium-high heat. Pour in 3 tablespoons of the olive oil and when the oil is hot, add the sweet potatoes, spreading them out into an even layer. Cook, tossing occasionally, until lightly browned, 4 to 6 minutes.

3. Add the remaining 1 tablespoon olive oil, the poblanos, onion, chipotle powder, cumin, salt, and a few grinds of black pepper. Cook, tossing occasionally, until the vegetables are browned and tender, 6 to 8 minutes, reducing the heat as necessary.

4. Add the garlic and 2 tablespoons of the scallions and cook for 1 more minute. Off the heat, stir in the vinegar, scraping up any browned bits from the bottom of the pan. Use a spoon to create 4 small hollows in the hash. Carefully crack an egg into each, and season the eggs with salt and pepper.

5. Carefully transfer the skillet to the oven and bake until the egg whites are just set, 5 to 7 minutes. (Be careful not to overcook the eggs.)

6. Sprinkle the cheese and the remaining 2 tablespoons scallions over the skillet. Serve hot with toast, sliced avocado, and, if using, hot sauce on the side. (A spatula works best for serving.)

Plum, Cardamom & Cornmeal Muffins

MAKES 12 MUFFINS

Nonstick cooking spray, as needed

1½ cups (195 grams) all-purpose flour

½ cup (70 grams) medium-grind or fine cornmeal

1½ teaspoons baking powder

½ teaspoon baking soda

½ teaspoon ground cardamom

¼ teaspoon ground cinnamon

⅛ teaspoon ground nutmeg

1 teaspoon kosher salt

1 cup (200 grams) granulated sugar

1 stick (4 ounces/113 grams) unsalted butter, melted and slightly cooled

2 large eggs, at room temperature

1 cup (240 grams) sour cream or plain Greek yogurt

1 teaspoon vanilla extract

Grated zest of 1 orange

2 large firm-ripe plums (about 9 ounces total), pitted

1 tablespoon demerara or turbinado sugar (optional)

TIP

Muffins will keep for three days, stored in a sealed container at room temperature. Place a paper towel in the container to help absorb any excess moisture.

Muffins are an easy homemade treat, and they have the added benefit of making your entire house smell like a bakery. (An especially impressive move to pull when you have houseguests for the weekend.)

These simple plum and cornmeal muffins are for my friend Lulu. We've shared many baked goods over the years, and now that we live across the country from each other, we have an unofficial tradition of making up for lost time and popping into as many bakeries as possible when we visit each other.

We had a delicious plum and cornmeal cake on my last visit to see Lulu in San Francisco, and I loved the combination of the coarse cornmeal with jammy baked plums. I've also added ground cardamom to give these muffins a fragrant aroma and subtle spiced flavor.

1. Preheat the oven to 375°F. Line a standard muffin tin with paper liners. (If you're not using a nonstick pan, spray the exposed metal with cooking spray so the muffin tops come out easily.)

2. In a medium bowl, whisk together the flour, cornmeal, baking powder, baking soda, cardamom, cinnamon, nutmeg, and salt. Set aside.

3. In a large bowl, combine the sugar, melted butter, and eggs. Whisk vigorously for about 15 seconds, until the yolks are pale and the mixture is smooth and glossy. Add the sour cream, vanilla, and orange zest and whisk just until smooth.

4. Add the dry ingredients to the wet ingredients and mix with a wooden spoon until just combined.

5. Cut the plums into ¼-inch dice. Measure out ⅓ cup and set aside, and fold the remainder into the batter. Using an ice cream scoop or large spoon, divide the batter among the 12 muffin cups. The cups will be very full. Spoon a few of the reserved diced plums onto each muffin and sprinkle the tops with the demerara sugar, if using. Wipe any excess sugar from the top of the pan.

6. Bake until a toothpick comes out clean and the muffins spring back when lightly pressed, 22 to 24 minutes.

7. Let the muffins cool completely in the pan before removing them. Serve at room temperature. Muffins are best the day they're made but will keep in a sealed container at room temperature for up to 3 days.

SIMPLE SWAP

While a juicy, super-ripe plum is ideal for eating, slightly underripe fruit makes for more evenly baked muffins. When plums aren't available or in season, try making these muffins with raspberries or chopped strawberries instead.

Red Potato & Leek Frittata with Goat Cheese & Dill

SERVES 6 TO 8

Softened unsalted butter for the baking dish

5 tablespoons olive oil, divided, plus more as needed

1 pound red potatoes (about 3 medium potatoes), scrubbed and ¼-inch diced

Kosher salt and freshly ground black pepper

2 large leeks, trimmed, halved lengthwise, and sliced ¼-inch thick (about 4 cups)

2 teaspoons white wine vinegar

12 large eggs

1 cup whole milk

1 (4-ounce) log plain goat cheese

2 tablespoons chopped fresh dill

A frittata is a great vehicle for whatever veggies you have in the fridge, but it also makes for a casual-yet-elegant brunch or lunch. I like to use red potatoes here, for a pop of color, and plenty of fresh dill. This frittata puffs up beautifully as it bakes, eliciting some nice "oohs and aahs" when it comes out of the oven. Serve hot for maximum fluffiness, or at room temperature if you're planning ahead. The frittata will deflate slightly as it cools but will still be delicious.

1. Preheat the oven to 350°F and generously butter a 9 × 13-inch baking dish.

2. In a 12-inch skillet, heat 3 tablespoons of the olive oil over medium-high heat. Add the potatoes, season with ½ teaspoon salt, and toss to coat. Spread them out into an even layer. Cook, tossing occasionally and scraping the bottom of the pan, until the potatoes are tender and lightly browned, about 10 minutes. Transfer the potatoes to the prepared baking dish.

3. Reduce the heat to medium. Add the remaining 2 tablespoons olive oil, the leeks, ½ teaspoon salt, and ½ teaspoon black pepper. Cook, tossing occasionally, until the leeks are lightly caramelized, 7 to 9 minutes. If the pan seems dry at any point, add a splash of oil.

4. Off the heat, add the vinegar and toss, scraping up any browned bits from the bottom of the pan. Transfer the leeks to the baking dish, toss with the potatoes, and spread everything into an even layer. Set aside.

5. In a large bowl, whisk together the eggs, milk, 1 teaspoon salt, and ½ teaspoon black pepper until smooth. Pour the egg mixture into the dish and give the dish a gentle shake to help distribute the eggs if necessary. Break the goat cheese into crumbles and scatter over the eggs, then sprinkle the dill on top.

6. Bake until the frittata is just set in the center, 25 to 30 minutes. Let sit for at least 10 minutes before serving. Serve warm or at room temperature.

Lidey Bars (Vegan Date & Almond Bars)

MAKES 12 BARS

1½ cups raw almonds (about 8 ounces), divided

3 cups pitted dates (15 ounces)

¼ teaspoon ground cinnamon

½ teaspoon kosher salt

1 cup unsweetened coconut flakes (about 2 ounces), divided

½ cup old-fashioned rolled oats (see Tip)

2 tablespoons extra-virgin olive oil

1 tablespoon maple syrup

TIP
Oats are naturally gluten-free but are often processed in facilities that handle flours and other grains. If you're avoiding gluten, make sure to use oats labeled "gluten-free."

When my neighbor in East Hampton, Denise Cara, ran the bakery at Amber Waves Farm, her delicious muffins and scones quickly developed a following. I stopped by often with friends for a coffee and a treat on the way to the beach, and if we were lucky, Denise would emerge from the kitchen with a tray of some freshly baked blueberry muffins or chocolate chip cookies for us to try. (My friend David Gruber happened to buy the one thousandth blueberry muffin of the summer and got his picture featured in the *East Hampton Star*, but that's a story for another time.)

One day, Denise was brainstorming ideas for something vegan and gluten-free, and I mentioned that I made date-nut bars that might fit the bill. She rolled with the idea, calling the bars "Lidey Bars" and adding a sprinkle of toasted coconut on top. The bars were a hit at Amber Waves, and when Denise eventually opened her own bakery in Rowayton, Connecticut, she kept them on the menu!

Made with dates, nuts, coconut, and oats, the bars are chewy and lightly sweet. And while you do need a food processor for these, don't let that deter you, because there really isn't much to the recipe. These are a great running-out-the-door breakfast or healthy snack to have on hand.

1. Preheat the oven to 350°F and line an 8 × 8-inch baking pan with parchment paper.

2. Place ¾ cup of the almonds in a food processor and process until coarsely chopped. Transfer to a large bowl and set aside.

3. Add the remaining ¾ cup almonds to the food processor and process until chopped. Add the dates, cinnamon, and salt and process until the mixture forms a coarse paste, 10 to 15 seconds. Add ⅔ cup of the coconut flakes, the oats, oil, and maple syrup and pulse until combined.

4. Dump the mixture out into the bowl with the almonds and mix until incorporated. The mixture should be sticky and dense. Transfer to the prepared pan and press into a flat even layer with a wooden spoon or the bottom of a measuring cup. Sprinkle the remaining ⅓ cup coconut on top, pressing gently so it adheres to the surface.

5. Bake until the coconut flakes and the edges of the bars are just beginning to brown, about 20 minutes. (Do not overbake.)

6. Cool completely, then cut into rectangular bars and serve. These bars are best eaten within 5 days. Store at room temperature in a sealed container.

Hummingbird Pancakes
with Caramelized Pineapple & Pecans

**MAKES 12 PANCAKES
(SERVES 4 TO 6)**

**For the caramelized
pineapple topping**

2 heaping cups (1-inch) cubes
fresh pineapple (about 12
ounces or one pineapple)

2 tablespoons unsalted butter

1 tablespoon maple syrup

½ cup pecans, coarsely
chopped

¼ teaspoon kosher salt

For the pancakes

1½ cups (195 grams) all-
purpose flour

2 teaspoons baking powder

1½ teaspoons ground
cinnamon

1 teaspoon kosher salt

1½ cups mashed ripe bananas
(about 3 medium bananas)

2 large eggs, lightly beaten

½ cup whole milk

2 tablespoons granulated
sugar

1 teaspoon vanilla extract

Unsalted butter, for frying

Maple syrup, for serving

These decadent pancakes are inspired by Hummingbird Cake, a moist spice
cake with bananas, pecans, and crushed pineapple that originated in Jamaica
in the 1960s and went on to become a popular dessert in the American South.
Instead of using canned crushed pineapple, I caramelize thin slices of fresh
pineapple in maple syrup before piling them onto the pancakes. They add a
deliciously sweet-tart tang I never knew pancakes were missing!

1. **First, make the caramelized pineapple:** Cut the pineapple cubes—cutting
with the "grain"—into ¼-inch-thick slices.

2. In a 12-inch nonstick skillet set over medium heat, combine the butter and
maple syrup, swirling the pan as the butter melts. When the mixture begins to
bubble and foam, add the pineapple and cook over medium-high heat, tossing
occasionally, until lightly caramelized, 4 to 6 minutes.

3. Reduce the heat to medium, add the pecans and salt and cook, tossing often,
until the nuts are toasted, 2 to 3 more minutes. Transfer the mixture to a bowl and
set aside. Rinse out the skillet and return it to the stove.

4. **Make the pancakes:** In a large bowl, whisk together the flour, baking powder,
cinnamon, and salt. In a medium bowl, combine the bananas, eggs, milk, sugar, and
vanilla and whisk until smooth. Add the wet ingredients to the dry ingredients and
mix with a wooden spoon until just combined. (There willl be some small lumps in
the batter.)

5. Place ½ tablespoon butter into the reserved skillet and heat it over medium-low
heat. Scoop ¼ cup pancake batter onto one side of the skillet and spread lightly
into a circle with the bottom of the measuring cup. Scoop out 2 more pancakes,
spacing them evenly in the pan. Cook until bubbles begin to form on top and
the bottoms are golden brown, about 2 minutes. Flip the pancakes and cook for
another minute. Transfer them to a serving platter. Repeat with the remaining
pancake batter, adjusting the heat so the pancakes brown evenly, and adding more
butter to the pan as necessary.

6. Serve the pancakes warm, with the pineapple and pecans and more maple
syrup.

MAKE IT A MEAL
Serve these for a special weekend breakfast, with bacon and
extra maple syrup on the side.

Dressings,
Sauces
& Extras

My go-to dressings and sauces, along with a few basic recipes that are staples in my kitchen.

Simple Lemon & Olive Oil Vinaigrette

MAKES ABOUT ½ CUP

2 tablespoons freshly squeezed lemon juice
(1 lemon)

½ teaspoon kosher salt

¼ teaspoon freshly ground black pepper

⅓ cup extra-virgin olive oil

In a small bowl or glass measuring cup, combine the lemon juice, salt, and pepper. Slowly whisk in the olive oil. This vinaigrette is best served within 24 hours. Store in a sealed container in the refrigerator.

Cider & Maple Vinaigrette

MAKES ¾ CUP

¼ cup apple cider vinegar

2 teaspoons maple syrup

1 teaspoon Dijon mustard

1 teaspoon kosher salt

¼ teaspoon freshly ground black pepper

½ cup extra-virgin olive oil

In a small bowl or glass measuring cup, combine the vinegar, maple syrup, mustard, salt, and pepper. Add the olive oil and whisk vigorously until smooth. Store in a sealed container in the refrigerator for up to 1 week.

Creamy Sesame Ginger Dressing

MAKES ½ CUP

3 tablespoons tahini

3 tablespoons extra-virgin olive oil

3 tablespoons seasoned rice vinegar

2 teaspoons grated fresh ginger

1 teaspoon soy sauce

1 small garlic clove, grated on a Microplane
(½ teaspoon)

½ teaspoon kosher salt

1 tablespoon cold water

In a small bowl or glass measuring cup, whisk together the tahini, olive oil, vinegar, ginger, soy sauce, garlic, and salt. Add the cold water and whisk until smooth and creamy. Store in a sealed container in the refrigerator for up to three days.

Greek Red Wine Vinaigrette

MAKES ½ CUP

6 tablespoons extra-virgin olive oil

2 tablespoons red wine vinegar

2 teaspoons minced garlic

½ teaspoon dried oregano

1 teaspoon kosher salt

¼ teaspoon freshly ground black pepper

In a small bowl or glass measuring cup, combine the olive oil, vinegar, garlic, oregano, salt, and pepper and whisk vigorously. Store in a sealed container in the refrigerator for up to 1 week.

Avocado Goddess Dressing

MAKES 1 CUP

1 teaspoon chopped garlic

3 tablespoons chopped fresh dill

2 tablespoons minced fresh chives or scallions (white and green parts)

1 Hass avocado (6 to 8 ounces), halved and pitted

½ cup mayonnaise

3 tablespoons freshly squeezed lemon juice (1 large lemon)

1 teaspoon kosher salt

Freshly ground black pepper

In a food processor, combine the garlic, dill, and chives and process until finely chopped. Scoop the avocado into the processor and add the mayonnaise, lemon juice, salt, and a few grinds of black pepper. Process until smooth, 10 to 15 seconds. Store in a sealed container in the refrigerator for up to 2 days before using.

Champagne Vinaigrette

MAKES ABOUT ⅓ CUP

¼ cup extra-virgin olive oil

1 tablespoon champagne vinegar or white wine vinegar

½ teaspoon Dijon mustard

¼ teaspoon kosher salt

Freshly ground black pepper

In a small bowl or glass measuring cup, combine the olive oil, vinegar, mustard, salt, and a few grinds of black pepper and whisk vigorously until smooth. Store in a sealed container in the refrigerator for up to 1 week.

Whole-Grain Mustard Vinaigrette

MAKES ½ CUP

2 tablespoons red wine vinegar

1 tablespoon minced shallots

1 teaspoon whole-grain mustard

1 teaspoon honey

¼ teaspoon kosher salt

Freshly ground black pepper

⅓ cup extra-virgin olive oil

In a small bowl or glass measuring cup, combine the vinegar, shallots, mustard, honey, salt, and a few grinds of black pepper and whisk together. Add the olive oil and whisk vigorously until smooth. Store in a sealed container in the refrigerator for up to three days.

Creamy Tahini-Yogurt Sauce

MAKES ABOUT 1 CUP

1 cup plain whole-milk yogurt

2 tablespoons tahini

1 tablespoon freshly squeezed lemon juice

½ medium garlic clove, grated or finely minced

¼ teaspoon kosher salt

In a medium bowl, combine the yogurt, tahini, lemon juice, garlic, and salt and mix well. Refrigerate for at least 30 minutes (and up to 3 days) in a sealed container before using.

Salsa Verde

MAKES ABOUT ½ CUP

3 tablespoons chopped fresh parsley

2 tablespoons chopped fresh mint

2 tablespoons capers, drained and coarsely chopped

2 tablespoons chopped scallion (about 1 scallion)

1 garlic clove, minced

2 tablespoons red wine vinegar or sherry vinegar

2 tablespoons extra-virgin olive oil

¼ teaspoon kosher salt

In a small bowl or glass measuring cup, combine the parsley, mint, capers, scallion, garlic, vinegar, olive oil, and salt and whisk to combine. Salsa verde is best served within 24 hours. Store in a sealed container in the refrigerator.

Quick-Pickled Red Onion

MAKES ABOUT 1½ CUPS

1½ cups packed thinly sliced red onion
(1 medium onion)

½ cup red wine vinegar

1 tablespoon granulated sugar

1 teaspoon kosher salt

1. Place the onions in a half-pint jar or other heatproof container and pack them lightly with a spoon.

2. In a small saucepan or skillet, combine the vinegar, ¼ cup water, the sugar, and salt. Bring to a simmer, stir to dissolve the sugar, then carefully pour the mixture over the onion.

3. Set aside until cool. Use immediately or refrigerate for up to 5 days before using.

Classic Cornbread

MAKES 9 SQUARES

6 tablespoons (3 ounces/85 grams) unsalted butter, melted, plus more for greasing the pan

1 cup (240 grams) whole milk

1 large egg

1 cup (130 grams) all-purpose flour

1 cup (140 grams) cornmeal

½ cup (100 grams) granulated sugar

1 tablespoon baking powder

1 teaspoon kosher salt

1. Preheat the oven to 400°F and grease an 8 × 8-inch baking dish with butter.

2. In a large bowl, whisk together the milk, melted butter, and egg. In a smaller bowl, combine the flour, cornmeal, sugar, baking powder, and salt. Add the dry ingredients to the wet ingredients and mix until just combined (some small lumps will remain). Pour the batter into the prepared pan.

3. Bake until the edges are beginning to brown and a toothpick comes out with just a few crumbs on it, 20 to 22 minutes. Cool slightly, then cut into squares and serve.

Skillet Croutons

MAKES 3 CUPS

3 tablespoons extra-virgin olive oil

3 cups cubed bread (about 4½ ounces)

Kosher salt

In a large skillet, heat the olive oil over medium heat. Add the bread cubes in a single layer and cook, tossing often, until browned all over, 3 to 5 minutes. Sprinkle with salt and transfer to a plate to cool.

Easy Garlic Baguette

SERVES 6

1 baguette, sliced lengthwise

5 tablespoons unsalted butter, at room temperature

¼ cup finely chopped fresh parsley

4 medium garlic cloves, grated on a Microplane

½ teaspoon kosher salt

⅓ cup grated Parmesan cheese

1. Preheat the oven to 400°F and line a sheet pan with foil or parchment paper.

2. Place the baguette halves on the lined sheet pan. In a small bowl, combine the butter, parsley, garlic, and salt. Mix with a fork until smooth. Spread over the cut sides of the bread with the butter and sprinkle with the Parmesan.

3. Bake until the bread is toasted and golden brown at the edges, about 15 minutes. Cut into pieces and serve hot.

Leftover-Chicken Chicken Broth

MAKES ABOUT 2 QUARTS

1 carcass from a roast chicken, any skin discarded

1 medium yellow onion, peeled and halved

4 garlic cloves, unpeeled

1 fresh rosemary sprig or 3 fresh thyme sprigs

Big handful of fresh dill or parsley (or both)

1 tablespoon kosher salt

1 teaspoon black peppercorns

1. In an 8-quart pot, combine the chicken carcass, onion, garlic, herbs, salt, peppercorns, and 16 cups water. Bring to a boil, then reduce the heat to a simmer and cook, uncovered, until the liquid is reduced by half, about 1½ hours.

2. Cool, then strain and discard the solids. Transfer the broth to freezer-safe 1-quart containers and refrigerate for up to 5 days or freeze for up to 3 months.

EASY ADD-ONS

The following ideas can turn almost any grain, salad, or side dish into a meal. Throughout the book, I've noted when I like to add a protein, such as roasted chicken breast or sautéed shrimp, to a salad or side to bulk it up for dinner, and what follows here are simple preparations for doing just that. By design, they require nothing more than olive oil (or butter), salt, and pepper.

Once you've made these basics a few times, you will expand your go-to repertoire exponentially. Feel free to make these recipes your own by adding a sprinkle of fresh herbs or your favorite seasonings—or drizzling with the dressings, sauces, and extras (starting on page 251), but know they are all delicious as written.

Roasted Chicken Breasts

MAKES ABOUT 3 CUPS SHREDDED CHICKEN

2 small bone-in, skin-on chicken breasts (about ¾ pound each)

2 tablespoons extra-virgin olive oil

Kosher salt and freshly ground black pepper

1. Preheat the oven to 350°F and line a sheet pan with parchment paper.

2. Pat the chicken breasts dry and place them on the lined pan. Drizzle the olive oil over the breasts, sprinkle with ½ teaspoon salt, and a few grinds of black pepper.

3. Roast until just cooked through (the internal temperature should be 165°F), 30 to 35 minutes.

4. Set aside until cool enough to handle, then shred or dice the chicken, discarding the skin and bones. Store in a sealed container in the refrigerator for up to 3 days.

Seared Salmon Fillets

SERVES 2 (EASILY DOUBLED)

2 skin-on salmon fillets (4 to 6 ounces each)

Extra-virgin olive oil

Kosher salt and freshly ground black pepper

1. Heat a large cast-iron or stainless steel skillet over medium-high heat until very hot (a drop of water flicked onto the pan should evaporate almost immediately).

2. Meanwhile, pat the salmon fillets dry with a paper towel and brush them all over with olive oil. Sprinkle generously with salt and black pepper.

3. Place the fillets, skin-side down, in the hot skillet and cook, without moving, until the skin releases easily, 3 to 4 minutes. Flip and cook until the fish is just cooked through and flakes easily, 3 to 5 more minutes, depending on the thickness of the fillets.

Sautéed Shrimp

SERVES 4 (EASILY HALVED)

1 pound shrimp (18/20 count) peeled and
deveined, tails on or off

Kosher salt and freshly ground black pepper

4 tablespoons extra-virgin olive oil or unsalted
butter

1. Pat the shrimp dry with a paper towel and place them in a
bowl. Sprinkle generously with salt and black pepper and toss.

2. In a large skillet, heat the olive oil or butter over medium
heat. Add the shrimp and cook, tossing often, until opaque and
just cooked through, about 3 minutes. Immediately transfer to a
plate to stop the cooking.

3. Serve hot, warm, or at room temperature.

Basic Roasted Potatoes

SERVES 4

1½ pounds small potatoes, such as Yukon Gold

2 tablespoons extra-virgin olive oil

Kosher salt and freshly ground black pepper

Chopped fresh dill or parsley (optional)

1. Preheat the oven to 425°F.

2. Cut the potatoes in half lengthwise and place on a sheet pan.
Drizzle with the olive oil and sprinkle with ½ teaspoon salt and a
few grinds of black pepper. Toss with your hands, then arrange
the potatoes so they are cut-sides down.

3. Roast until browned and crisp on the cut sides and tender
when pierced with a fork, 30 to 35 minutes, depending on the
size of the potatoes. Sprinkle with salt. If desired, garnish with
fresh dill. Serve hot, warm, or at room temperature.

Simple Green Salad

SERVES 4

1 (5-ounce) container arugula, mixed greens, or
chopped kale (about 8 handfuls or cups)

⅓ cup dressing of your choice (recipes on pages
254–256)

Optional add-ins: Handful of chopped nuts,
fresh herbs, chopped cucumber, bell pepper,
tomatoes, or leftover roasted veggies

Kosher salt and freshly ground black pepper

Wash and dry the greens and put them in a very large bowl.
Drizzle the dressing over the greens and toss gently but
thoroughly. Add any desired add-ins. Season with salt and black
pepper and serve.

Menus

Busy Weeknight for 1, 2, or 4
Salmon with Honey & Chili Crunch (page 122)

Steamed rice

Side of Greens with Garlic & Soy (page 150)

Brunch Party
English Muffin Breakfast Bake (page 232) or Red Potato
   & Leek Frittata with Goat Cheese & Dill (page 245)

Winter Fruit Salad (page 235)

Garibaldi Spritz (page 42)

Plum, Cardamom & Cornmeal Muffins (page 242)

Festive Holiday Dinner
Brown Bread Crackers with Crème Fraîche & Smoked
   Salmon (page 37)

Baked Harbison (page 29)

Celery Waldorf with Pickled Golden Raisins (page 69)

Braised Short Ribs with Port, Shallots & Cranberries
   (page 111)

Creamy Polenta (page 162)

Candy's Flourless Chocolate Cake (page 211)—with
   candy canes!

Summer Grilling
Grilled Skirt Steak with Romesco Salsa (page 102)

Grilled Zucchini with Charred Lemon Dressing, Feta
   & Mint (page 178)

Coconut Creamed Corn (page 182)

Peaches & Cream Pie (page 204)

End of Summer Blowout
Cherry, Nectarine & Jalapeño Salsa (page 45)

Spicy Paloma Punch (page 22)

Spaghetti with Sweet Corn Pesto (page 138)

Simple Green Salad (page 263)

Ice cream sundaes!

Breakfast, PJs & Reality TV
Sweet Potato & Poblano Hash with Eggs (page 241)

Winter Fruit Salad (page 235)

Coffee

Dinner for Vegan Friends
Crispy Cauliflower & Chickpea Cakes with Moroccan
   Spices (page 142), made with nondairy yogurt

Simple Green Salad (page 263)

Crispy Smashed Potatoes with Salsa Verde (page 181)

Extra harissa, for serving

Fancy Spring Lunch (or Dinner)
Slow-Roasted Salmon with Lemony Leeks & Asparagus
   (page 126)

Simply cooked farro

Arugula & Romaine Salad with Radish, Shaved Parm,
   Pistachios & Mint (page 73)

Strawberry Rhubarb Shortcake with Buttermilk Biscuits
   (page 195)

Cozy Winter Dinner
Orecchiette with White Bolognese (page 101)

Green Beans with Crispy Capers & Garlic (page 157)

Perfect Little Chocolate Puddings (page 200)

Movie Night/Dinner on the Coffee Table
Saucy Shrimp alla Vodka (page 118)

Roasted Broccolini with Pickled Pepperoncini (page 172)

Easy Garlic Baguette (page 259)

Movie theater candy

Bistro Night Chez Vous

White Bean & Mushroom Cassoulet with Gruyère Bread Crumbs (page 132)

Asparagus Vinaigrette (page 165)

Roasted Pears with Brandy & Brown Sugar (page 217)

All Apples Fall Dinner

Cider & Bourbon Old-Fashioned (page 30)

Kale Salad with Gouda, Honeycrisp & Walnuts (page 50)

Cider-Glazed Sausages with Caramelized Apples & Fennel (page 87)

Skillet Apple Crisp with Shortbread Crumble (page 218)

All-Out BBQ

Cherry, Nectarine & Jalapeño Salsa (page 45) with corn chips

Spicy Barbecue Pulled Chicken Sandwiches (page 96)

Potato & Chickpea Salad with Dill & Cornichons (page 174)

Perfect Picnic Coleslaw (page 170)

Almost-Famous 4th of July Ice Cream Sandwiches (page 207)

Celebratory Dinner at Home

Baked Harbison (page 29)

Champagne Chicken (page 88)

Warm Herbed Farro (page 154)

Escarole Salad with Cara Cara Oranges, Marcona Almonds & Goat Cheese (page 57)

Banana Cake with Dark Chocolate Frosting & Sea Salt (page 192)

Weeknight "Fancy" Dinner

Roast Chicken with Cipollini Onions, White Beans & Lemon (page 106)

Kale Salad with Gouda, Honeycrisp & Walnuts (page 50)

Dinner at the Beach

Baked Crab Dip with Sweet Corn & Old Bay (page 41)

Littleneck Clams with Cherry Tomatoes & Pearl Couscous (page 125)

Crusty bread

Simple Green Salad (page 263)

Ice cream straight from the pint

Dinner Party for Nervous Cooks

Roasted Fish with Green Herbs, Lemon & Olives (page 121)

Cooked farro or brown rice

Arugula & Romaine Salad with Radish, Shaved Parm, Pistachios & Mint (page 73)

Ask a friend to bring dessert!

Cooking with/for Kiddos

One-Pan Chicken Meatballs with Red Sauce & Spinach (page 84)

Creamy Polenta (page 162)

Rainbow Sprinkle Ice Cream Cake (page 213)

Hot Date Night In

Gin Martini with Rosemary & Grapefruit (page 38)

Date-Night Rib Eye with Wild Mushrooms (page 91)

Crispy Smashed Potatoes with Salsa Verde (page 181)

Dirty Blondies with Chocolate, Hazelnut & Coffee (page 199)

Summer Heat Wave

Beach Water (page 34)

Melon & Cucumber Gazpacho (page 70)

Tomato & Peach Salad with Toasted Farro & Mozzarella (page 78)

Simple Green Salad (page 263)

Cozy Lunch at Home

Radicchio Salad with Pear, Cornbread Crumbs & Bacon (page 77)

Peanut Butter & Ginger Cookies (page 190)

Sources

One of the best parts of doing the photographs for this book was getting to feature some of my favorite serving pieces and table linens. I'm excited to share this reference list—I hope it provides you with inspiration and ideas for your own home and kitchen!

If an item is missing from the list, it may be because many of the pieces are vintage. I'm always on the hunt for vintage tabletop items , but a few of my favorite places to shop for them are thrift shops, antique stores, and flea markets. I've shared sources here when possible. Online, I love to peruse Etsy, eBay, and Facebook Marketplace for unique finds.

page 23 glass pitcher/CB2

page 27 china side plates/vintage

page 28 mini oval baker/All-Clad

page 31 rocks glass/Nude Glass

page 32 pink glass bowl/vintage

page 35 glass pitcher/Juniper (Millbrook, NY)

page 36 platter/DBO Home

page 39 martini glass/vintage

page 40 baking dish/Judy Jackson Stoneware

page 43 glasses/Il Buco Vita

page 44 salsa bowl/Jan Burtz; blue-rimmed plate/Canvas Home

page 51 salad servers/Sabre Paris

page 52 pot/vintage; bowls/Hammertown; kitchen towel/Caravan

page 55 bowl, vintage enamelware/Hammertown (Pine Plains, NY)

page 56 plates/The Platera; forks/Sabre Paris, fabric/Schuyler Samperton

page 59 tablecloth/Solino Home

page 60 platter/DBO Home

page 63 bowl/vintage china

page 64 bowl Il Buco Vita; napkin/Heather Taylor Home

page 68 platter/vintage ironstone via Etsy; napkin/Hammertown (Pine Plains, New York)

page 71 bowls/DBO Home

page 72 bowl/Canvas Home; napkin/Heather Taylor Home

page 75 plate/Terrain; soup bowl/Canvas Home

page 76 platter/vintage; linen table runner/Anthropologie

page 79 platter/vintage; napkin/The Lost Kitchen shop

page 86 skillet/vintage enameled cast-iron; napkin/Crate & Barrel

page 89 platter/vintage; runner/Minna Goods

page 90 skillet/All-Clad

page 95 platter/Canvas Home; tablecloth/Linen Me

page 100 bowls/vintage; flatware and napkin/Hammertown

page 103 platter/Elephant Ceramics; small blue dish/vintage

page 107 napkin/Heather Taylor Home

page 109 plate/Falcon Enamelware; flatware/Sabre Paris; textile/Les Indiennes

page 110 tablecloth/Heather Taylor home; flatware/Sabre Paris

page 119 plate/Fish's Eddy; glass/Nude Glass

page 120 platter/vintage Bennington Pottery

page 123 plate/Jan Burtz

page 124 bowl/DBO Home

page 127 tablecloth/Schuyler Samperton fabric; flatware/Sabre Paris

page 133 Dutch oven/Dansk; plate/vintage

page 136 napkin/Heather Taylor Home

page 139 bowl/vintage

page 140 bowls/Canvas Home

page 143 plate/Judy Jackson Stoneware; napkin/Hammertown

page 151 napkin/Lost Kitchen Shop

page 152 vintage ironstone platter/Hammertown

page 156 platter/vintage; tablecloth/Estremi Roma

Acknowledgments

Writing a cookbook may sound like a solitary pursuit, but it's really the culmination of years of shared meals, stories, late nights at the dinner table, kitchen experiments, and a thousand conversations about food and recipes. I could not have written this book without help and guidance from mentors, collaborators, and friends, as well as the incredible team who worked closely with me throughout this entire process. Thank you all, from the bottom of my heart, for helping me bring these pages to life!

First, to Ina Garten. Thank you for your endless support— for introducing me to a world of possibility, for encouraging me as I found my own path, and for teaching me the importance of a well-written, well-tested recipe. You changed my life, and I will be forever grateful.

To my editor, Doris Cooper. Thank you for being the first and most ardent supporter of this book, for pushing me to find my voice, and for poring over these recipes with me into the wee hours. To Richard Rhorer, for trusting my vision, to Katie McClimon, for keeping everything organized, and to Patrick Sullivan, Laura Jarrett, Jessica Preeg, Elizabeth Breeden, and the the entire team at Simon & Schuster / Simon Element for your hard work and dedication to this project. And to Laura Palese, who designed these stunning pages!

To my agent, Kari Stuart. We finally did it! Thank you, thank you for being in my corner.

To my super-star photo team: Dane Tashima, Jane Gaspar, Nora Singley, Alyssa Kondracki, and Pam Morris. Thank you for bringing my recipes to life. Shooting these photos with you was a joy and a privilege!

To Lisa Nicklin, who tested each and every recipe. Thank you for your attention to detail and for being the only person I know who could discuss the weight of 1 cup of brown sugar with me 'til the cows come home.

To Sam Sifton, Emily Weinstein, Genevieve Ko, Margaux Laskey, Alexa Weibel, Cathy Lo, Melissa Knific, Priya Krishna, and everyone on the *New York Times Cooking* team. It's an honor and a dream to work with you.

To Erin French and Michael Dutton. I am endlessly grateful for your friendship, guidance, and loyalty.

To Molly Yeh, Jennifer Segal, Odette Williams, and Dan Pelosi, for your support and kind words about this book.

To Anthropologie, Terrain, Le Creuset, Sezane, Heather Taylor Home, Sabre Paris, Joan Osofsky of Hammertown, Dana Brandwein of DBO Home, Dana and Fritz Rohn of Montage Antiques, and Schuyler Samperton for lending and gifting beautiful cookware, serving pieces, kitchen linens and wardrobe for the photos in this book. And to Ellie Limpert and Romane Recalde for filling these pages with your gorgeous flowers.

To the friends and cheerleaders, who have advised, supported, and shared wisdom both professional and personal over the years: Nancy and Chris Kelley, Wendy Wurtzburger, Barbara Libath, Anne Erni, Kate Tyler, Kristina Felix, Colu Henry, Daisy Zeijlon, Nicole Franzen, Jessie Sheehan, Kerry Diamond, Saied Abbasi, Jake Cohen, Pam Lewy, Abena Anim-Somuah, Mary Giuliani, Courtney White, Denise Cara, Katie Baldwin, Amanda Merrow, Martha Oakes, Clare deBoer, and Brian Levy.

To the pals who fill my table with laughter and love, especially Julia Graham, Simon Bordwin, Louisa Reis, Ali Fradin, Louisa Cannell, Molly Fisher, Elizabeth Grimes, Emma Millard, Liza LePage, Helen Renninger, Paul Weinstein, Peyton Kelley, Roxanne Stewart, Devon Rosenstock, Maggie Woodward, Stanton Plummer-Cambridge, David Gruber, Marguerite Mariscal, Emily Graham, David Shaeffer, Claire Collery, Morgan Estey, Danny Chaffetz, Chris Omachi, Megan Garwood, & Maia Jaidi.

To my Pittsburgh, Bowdoin, East Hampton, Hudson Valley, and Les Cheneaux communities, for your support and excitement for this book! And to my online community—the friends I haven't met yet—this book has been in the works for a long time and could not have succeeded without you!

To my mom and dad, for always encouraging me to work hard, take risks, and have fun. To Sam, Kate, and Henry for putting up with my messes and enthusiastically eating hot soup in July. To my extended Heuck and Uricchio fam (especially Mike, Candy, Robert, and Nina), and my Piscina fam, Joe, Mary, Tom, Julie, Allie, and Nonna. Thank you all for being part of this journey, for sharing input and family recipes, and for supporting me through it all.

And finally to my husband, Joe, who did load after load of dishes, went on countless grocery runs, and who is always, *always*, my number one taste tester. I love you, and I could not have written a cookbook without you. We know this!

Index